THE COCKTAIL BAR

THE COCKTAIL BAR

By
"CHARLES"

Edited by
"CARLOS"

LONDON
W. FOULSHAM & CO. LTD.
NEW YORK   TORONTO   CAPE TOWN   SYDNEY

W. FOULSHAM & CO. LTD.,
Bennetts Close, Cippenham, Berkshire, SL1 5AP

0-572-00995-**X**

© *W. FOULSHAM & CO. LTD. 1977*

Printed in Great Britain by
St Edmundsbury Press Ltd, Bury St Edmunds, Suffolk

PREFACE

OUR object in compiling this book has been to provide instructions for mixing a wide variety of cocktails and other drinks. We have included all the popular ones, and also some that are less well known but deserve wider recognition.

Even some of the old favourites are mixed in different ways in different bars, because individual taste varies quite a lot. Both of us have been experimenting for years, and the recipes we have given here are the ones that we have found to be the most popular.

"CHARLES" and "CARLOS"

CONTENTS

CHAPTER I

CHAPTER II

COCKTAILS

8

CHAPTER III

AMERICAN AND OTHER SUMMER DRINKS

COBBLERS

COOLERS

CRUSTAS

Bacardi Crusta	88
Brandy Crusta	88
Gin Crusta	88
Rum Crusta	89
Whisky Crusta	89

DAISIES

Brandy Daisy	89
Gin Daisy	89
Rum Daisy	90
Whisky Daisy	90
White Horse Daisy	90

FIXES

Brandy Fix	90
Gin Fix	91
Rum Fix	91
Whisky Fix	91

FIZZES

Angostura Fizz	91
Brandy Fizz	91
Cream Fizz	91
Gin Fizz	92
Golden Fizz	92
Morning Glory Fizz	92
Orange Fizz	92
Royal Fizz	92
Rum Fizz	92
Rye Fizz	92
Silver Fizz	93

HIGHBALLS

Applejack Highball	93
Brandy Highball	93
Gin Highball	93
Rum Highball	93
Sherry Highball	93
Vermouth Highball	93
Whisky Highball	93

MINT JULEPS

Brandy Julep (1)	94
Brandy Julep (2)	94
Brandy Julep (3)	94
Champagne Julep	95
Gin Julep	95
Rum Julep	95
Whisky Julep	95

RICKEYS

Applejack Rickey	95
Brandy Rickey	95
Gin Rickey	95
Rum Rickey	96
Sloe Gin Rickey	96
Whisky Rickey	96

SANGAREES

Ale Sangaree	96
Port Wine Sangaree	96
Sherry Sangaree	97
Whisky Sangaree	97

SLINGS

Gin Sling	97
Rum Sling	97
Singapore Sling	97
Straits Sling	98
Whisky Sling	98

SMASHES

Brandy Smash	98
Gin Smash	98
Rum Smash	98
Whisky Smash	99

SOURS

Applejack Sour	99
Brandy Sour	99
Gin Sour	99
Rum Sour	99
Whisky Sour	99

CHAPTER IV

CUPS AND PUNCHES

CHAPTER V

SUMMER BEVERAGES (NON-ALCOHOLIC)

LEMONADES, ORANGEADES, ETC.

CHAPTER VI

EGG NOGGS, FLIPS, AND MILK PUNCHES

EGG NOGGS

FLIPS AND OTHER EGG DRINKS

MILK PUNCH AND OTHER DRINKS

CHAPTER VII

HOT DRINKS

PUNCHES

TODDIES

OTHER HOT DRINKS

COFFEES

CHAPTER VIII

MISCELLANEOUS DRINKS

APÉRITIFS

POUSSE CAFÉS

19

CHAPTER IX

Chapter I

THE COCKTAIL CABINET

THE professional cocktail mixer is sometimes thought of as a sort of magician, who compounds his recipes according to secret formulae and produces delicious drinks that no amateur could hope to equal. In fact this is very far from the truth. Mixing cocktails is more of a science than an art – and the first principles are easily learnt. With a little knowledge and ordinary care any amateur can soon learn to prepare cocktails and other drinks that will delight the most discriminating palate.

A cocktail cabinet is an article of furniture, and of course one does not need a cabinet in order to be able to prepare cocktails. Modern sideboards are often made with special cocktail compartments, and these are quite adequate for the purpose. All that is needed is somewhere to keep the equipment and stock handy for use.

The basic equipment needed is as follows:

1. A shaker. This looks something like a miniature Thermos flask, and consists simply of two nickel containers that fit into each other.

2. A mixing glass. This is simply a large tumbler or bar glass.

3. A mixing spoon. This is a spoon holding about the same amount as a teaspoon, but with a long, thin handle.

4. A strainer.

5. A lemon squeezer.

6. A muddler. This is an implement used for crushing sugar or bruising fruit, mint, etc.

7. A gill measure graded with various fractional parts.

The above are the essentials. Of the other forms of equipment many are part of the normal culinary equipment. Obviously a corkscrew and bottle opener are required, and for certain recipes a nutmeg grater will be needed. A fruit knife and a fork and spoon for handling fruit will be wanted, too, and there should be an ice pick and a scoop or tongs for handling ice. Finally straws are needed for the longer drinks, and a bundle of cherry sticks to allow simple manipulation of the cherries, olives, etc., that are served in certain cocktails.

Decanter bottles with stoppers are desirable for ingredients that have to be served in the small measurements known as dashes.

Finally there are the glasses, and it is important to learn the measurements of capacity of these. All these measurements are reckoned in fractions of a gill, which is one-quarter of a pint. The glasses required are as follows:

1. Cocktail glasses. Each holds about $\frac{1}{2}$ gill.
2. Small wine-glasses. Each holds about $\frac{3}{4}$ gill.
3. Wine-glasses. Each holds about 1 gill.
4. Tumblers. Each holds about $\frac{1}{2}$ pint, or 2 gills.
5. Liqueur glasses. Each holds about $\frac{1}{4}$ gill. However, fine liqueurs are generally served in large "balloon" glasses. For ordinary purposes a half-filled cocktail glass is suitable for the serving of a liqueur.
6. Pousse café glasses. Also known as *petites flutes*. Each holds about $\frac{3}{8}$ gill.

The next thing to be considered after the equipment is the stock. A full list of all the different ingredients used in cocktails and similar drinks would be rather alarming, and in any case a stock of this size is quite unnecessary for the home cocktail cabinet. The following ingredients will allow the mixer plenty of scope, enabling him to prepare a wide variety of drinks:

1. A bottle of dry gin.
2. A bottle of Scotch whisky.
3. A bottle of brandy.
4. A bottle of French vermouth.
5. A bottle of Italian vermouth.
6. A bottle of dry sherry.
7. A small bottle of Angostura bitters.

8. A small bottle of orange bitters.
9. A half-bottle of curaçao.
10. A half-bottle of maraschino.
11. A bottle of grenadine.

For sweetening, plain sugar syrup or gum syrup is preferable to sugar, although certain recipes are always prepared with sugar. Soda water is needed for many summer drinks.

In recipes where milk is used it must be unboiled and should be rich. Eggs must always be very fresh.

It is important that all the ingredients used should be of good quality. It is not possible to make a good cocktail out of inferior materials.

The list of suggested ingredients above may appear rather formidable. However, while it is not a maximum stock it is not a minimum either, and many good drinks can be prepared with a smaller stock. The important thing to remember is that while the outlay may be larger, preparing cocktails is no more expensive in the long run than preparing simpler drinks, for the quantities used are small.

The first thing the cocktail mixer should bear in mind is to follow the recipe. He must not guess, and he must always measure exactly. Bitters and syrups especially must be used with great care, as even a slight error in measurement may spoil the drink.

Unless otherwise stated, the measurements in each recipe are calculated to provide a single drink. Thus, for example, the measurements in each cocktail recipe add up to half a gill, the capacity of the cocktail glass.

A "dash" (for example, of bitters or syrup) is equivalent to about one-third of a teaspoonful. Put another way, there are about fifty dashes to half a gill, the capacity of the cocktail glass.

Shaking should be done with both hands, briskly and thoroughly, until the ingredients are properly mixed and cooled.

Certain ingredients – champagne, for example – must not be shaken, and in many recipes drinks are stirred (with the mixing spoon) in the mixing glass. Unless the recipe states that the stirring should be gentle, it should be done quite briskly, the mixing spoon being whirled round until the ingredients are properly mixed and cooled.

Unless special instructions are given in the recipe, the order in which the ingredients are put into the shaker or mixing glass is not of great importance.

Most of the drinks in this book require the use of ice. This must be absolutely clean and should not be touched by hand. Fruits should not be handled either, and should be kept in a cool place until required.

In some recipes lemon peel is required to be squeezed on top of the drink. For this, a thin piece of peel should be taken between the fingers and gently squeezed or twisted, so that the juice drops into the drink. The lemon peel should never be put in the glass unless it is required by the recipe.

Chapter II

COCKTAILS

Note: In each recipe in this chapter it is stated whether the shaker or the mixing glass should be used. Unless special instructions are given, the following methods should always be used:

With the shaker: Half fill with broken ice, add the ingredients, shake well, and strain into a cocktail glass.

With the mixing glass: Half fill with broken ice, stir up well with the mixing spoon, and strain into a cocktail glass.

Addington Cocktail

$\frac{1}{4}$ *gill of French vermouth,*
$\frac{1}{4}$ *gill of Italian vermouth.*

Use the mixing glass. Serve in a wine-glass, top with soda, and squeeze a little orange-peel juice on top.

Adonis Cocktail

1 *dash of orange bitters,*
$\frac{1}{3}$ *gill of dry sherry,*
$\frac{1}{6}$ *gill of Italian vermouth.*

Use the mixing glass.

Affinity Cocktail

2 *dashes of Angostura bitters,*
$\frac{1}{6}$ *gill of French vermouth,*
$\frac{1}{6}$ *gill of Italian vermouth,*
$\frac{1}{6}$ *gill of Scotch whisky.*

Use the mixing glass. Serve with a cherry and a little lemon-peel juice squeezed on top.

After Dinner Cocktail (1)

The juice and rind of one lime,
¼ gill of apricot brandy,
¼ gill of Cointreau.
Use the shaker.

After Dinner Cocktail (2)

4 dashes of lemon juice,
¼ gill of cherry brandy,
¼ gill of prunelle brandy.
Use the shaker.

After Supper Cocktail

4 dashes of fresh lemon juice,
¼ gill of Cointreau,
¼ gill of apricot brandy.
Use the shaker.

Alaska Cocktail

2 dashes of orange bitters,
⅛ gill of yellow Chartreuse,
⅜ gill of dry gin.
Use the shaker. Serve with a little lemon-peel juice squeezed on top.

Alexander Cocktail (1)

⅛ gill of crème de cacao,
⅛ gill of sweet cream,
¼ gill of dry gin.
Use the shaker.

Alexander Cocktail (2)

$\frac{1}{6}$ *gill of crème de cacao,*
$\frac{1}{6}$ *gill of sweet cream,*
$\frac{1}{6}$ *gill of brandy.*
Use the shaker.

Alexander's Sister Cocktail

$\frac{1}{8}$ *gill of crème de menthe,*
$\frac{1}{8}$ *gill of sweet cream,*
$\frac{1}{4}$ *gill of dry gin.*
Use the shaker.

Alfonso Cocktail

1 *lump of sugar,*
2 *dashes of Secrestat bitter,*
$\frac{1}{2}$ *gill of Dubonnet,*
$\frac{1}{2}$ *gill of champagne.*
Put the lump of sugar in a wine-glass, and add the Secrestat bitter. Then add one lump of ice and the Dubonnet and stir gently. Fill up with champagne, and serve with a little lemon-peel juice squeezed on top.

Alice Mine Cocktail

2 *dashes of Scotch whisky,*
$\frac{1}{4}$ *gill of Italian vermouth,*
$\frac{1}{4}$ *gill of kummel.*
Use the mixing glass.

Allen (special) Cocktail

1 *dash of lemon juice,*
$\frac{1}{6}$ *gill of maraschino,*
$\frac{1}{3}$ *gill of Plymouth gin.*
Use the shaker.

Allies Cocktail

> 2 *dashes of kummel,*
> $\frac{1}{4}$ *gill of French vermouth,*
> $\frac{1}{4}$ *gill of dry gin.*

Use the shaker.

American Beauty Cocktail

> 1 *dash of crème de menthe,*
> $\frac{1}{8}$ *gill of fresh orange juice,*
> $\frac{1}{8}$ *gill of grenadine,*
> $\frac{1}{8}$ *gill of French vermouth,*
> $\frac{1}{8}$ *gill of brandy.*

Use the shaker. Serve with a little port wine on top.

Americano Cocktail

> $\frac{1}{6}$ *gill of Campari,*
> $\frac{1}{6}$ *gill of sweet vermouth – stir and fill with soda.*

Serve with ice. Add twist of lemon peel.

Angel Face Cocktail

> $\frac{1}{6}$ *gill of apricot brandy,*
> $\frac{1}{6}$ *gill of calvados,*
> $\frac{1}{6}$ *gill of dry gin.*

Use the shaker.

Angel's Tip Cocktail

> $\frac{1}{3}$ *gill of crème de cacao,*
> $\frac{1}{9}$ *gill of fresh cream.*

Float cream on top.

Aperitifs

See page 119.

Appetizer Cocktail

1 *dash of absinthe,*
$\frac{1}{4}$ *gill of Dubonnet,*
$\frac{1}{4}$ *gill of dry gin.*

Use the shaker. Serve with a little lemon-peel juice squeezed on top.

Applejack Rabbit Cocktail

For four persons:
$\frac{1}{3}$ *gill of fresh lemon juice,*
$\frac{1}{3}$ *gill of fresh orange juice,*
$\frac{2}{3}$ *gill of maple syrup,*
$\frac{2}{3}$ *gill of applejack brandy.*

Use the shaker.

Apple Pie Cocktail

2 *dashes of apricot brandy,*
$\frac{1}{4}$ *gill of bacardi rum,*
$\frac{1}{4}$ *gill of Italian vermouth.*

Use the shaker.

Approve Cocktail

2 *dashes of Angostura bitters,*
2 *dashes of Cointreau,*
$\frac{1}{2}$ *gill of Canadian Club whisky.*

Use the mixing glass. Serve with a little lemon-peel juice squeezed on top.

Artist's Special Cocktail

For four persons:
$\frac{1}{3}$ *gill of fresh lemon juice,*
$\frac{1}{3}$ *gill of gooseberry syrup,*
$\frac{2}{3}$ *gill of dry sherry,*
$\frac{2}{3}$ *gill of Scotch whisky.*

Use the mixing glass.

Astoria Cocktail (1)

1 dash of orange bitters,
⅙ gill of French vermouth,
⅓ gill of dry gin.

Use the mixing glass. Serve with a stuffed olive.

Astoria Cocktail (2)

1 dash of orange bitters,
½ gill of applejack brandy.

Use the shaker.

Atta Boy Cocktail

4 dashes of grenadine,
⅙ gill of French vermouth,
⅓ gill of dry gin.

Use the shaker. Serve with a little lemon-peel juice squeezed on top.

Aviation Cocktail

2 dashes of maraschino,
⅙ gill of fresh lemon juice,
⅓ gill of dry gin.

Use the shaker.

Bacardi Cocktail

⅙ gill of fresh lime juice,
⅓ gill of bacardi rum,
Sugar syrup to taste.

Use the shaker.

Bacardi Special Cocktail

1 teaspoonful of grenadine,
The juice of half a lime,
⅙ gill of dry gin,
⅓ gill of bacardi rum.

Use the shaker.

Balalaika Cocktail

$\frac{1}{6}$ *gill of vodka,*
$\frac{1}{6}$ *gill of Cointreau,*
$\frac{1}{6}$ *gill of lemon juice.*
Use the shaker.

Bamboo or Reform Cocktail (1)

1 *dash of Angostura bitters,*
$\frac{1}{4}$ *gill of dry sherry,*
$\frac{1}{4}$ *gill of Italian vermouth.*
Use the mixing glass. Serve with a little lemon-peel juice squeezed on top.

Bamboo or Reform Cocktail (2)

1 *dash of orange bitters,*
$\frac{1}{4}$ *gill of dry sherry,*
$\frac{1}{4}$ *gill of French vermouth.*
Use the mixing glass. Serve with a little lemon-peel juice squeezed on top.

Belmont Cocktail

1 *teaspoonful of sweet cream,*
$\frac{1}{6}$ *gill of grenadine,*
$\frac{1}{3}$ *gill of dry gin.*
Use the shaker.

Bennett Cocktail

2 *dashes of Angostura bitters,*
$\frac{1}{3}$ *gill of dry gin,*
$\frac{1}{6}$ *gill of lime juice.*
Use the shaker.

Bentley Cocktail

$\frac{1}{4}$ *gill of Dubonnet,*
$\frac{1}{4}$ *gill of calvados.*
Use the shaker.

Bermudian Rose Cocktail

$\frac{1}{3}$ *gill of dry gin,*
$\frac{1}{6}$ *gill of apricot brandy,*
$\frac{1}{6}$ *gill of grenadine,*
$\frac{1}{6}$ *gill of lemon juice.*
Use the shaker.

Between the Sheets Cocktail

1 *dash of fresh lemon juice,*
$\frac{1}{6}$ *gill of Cointreau,*
$\frac{1}{6}$ *gill of brandy,*
$\frac{1}{6}$ *gill of bacardi rum.*
Use the shaker.

Bijou Cocktail

1 *dash of orange bitters,*
$\frac{1}{6}$ *gill of Plymouth gin,*
$\frac{1}{6}$ *gill of green Chartreuse,*
$\frac{1}{6}$ *gill of Italian vermouth.*
Use the mixing glass. Serve with a cherry and a little lemon-peel
juice squeezed on top.

Black Russia Cocktail

$\frac{1}{6}$ *gill of vodka,*
$\frac{1}{6}$ *gill of kalhua.*
Stir and serve on ice.

Blackthorn Cocktail

2 *dashes of orange bitters,*
$\frac{1}{6}$ *gill of Italian vermouth,*
$\frac{1}{6}$ *gill of French vermouth,*
$\frac{1}{6}$ *gill of sloe gin.*
Use the mixing glass. Serve with a cherry and a little lemon-peel
juice squeezed on top.

 From left: Hot Gin (116), Gimlet (45), Bulldog Cooler (86), Pink Lady Cocktail (63), Orange Blossom Cocktail (1) (60), Grape Vine Cocktail (46), Cream Fizz (91).

Clockwise from left: Cider Cocktail (81), Alfonso Cocktail (27), Dubonnet Cocktail (43), Angostura Fizz (91), Gin Sling (97), Café Royal Appetiser Cocktail (36), Royal Cocktail (centre) (67).

Black Velvet Cocktail

Half cold Guinness,
Half chilled dry champagne.
Serve in ½ pint or 1 pint measures; add Guinness to champagne.

Blenton Cocktail

1 *dash of Angostura bitters,*
⅙ *gill of French (or dry Martini) vermouth,*
⅓ *gill of Plymouth gin.*
Use the shaker. Serve with a cherry and a little lemon-peel juice
squeezed on top.

Blood and Sand Cocktail

⅛ *gill of fresh orange juice,*
⅛ *gill of Italian vermouth,*
⅛ *gill of cherry brandy,*
⅛ *gill of Scotch whisky.*
Use the mixing glass.

Bloodhound Cocktail (1)

3 *crushed strawberries,*
⅛ *gill of French vermouth,*
⅛ *gill of Italian vermouth,*
¼ *gill of dry gin.*
Use the shaker.

Bloodhound Cocktail (2)

6 *crushed strawberries,*
2 *dashes of maraschino,*
⅛ *gill of French vermouth,*
⅛ *gill of Italian vermouth,*
¼ *gill of dry gin.*
Use the shaker.

Bloody Mary Cocktail

⅓ *gill of vodka,*
2 *dashes of Worcester sauce,*
Little lemon juice,
Tomato juice.

Use 6 oz. goblet. Add ice, vodka, Worcester sauce, a little lemon juice. Top with tomato juice and stir.

Blue Bird Cocktail

4 *dashes of Angostura bitters,*
5 *dashes of orange curaçao,*
½ *gill of dry gin.*

Use the shaker. Serve with a cherry and a little lemon-peel juice squeezed on top.

Bobby Burns Cocktail

3 *dashes of Bénédictine,*
¼ *gill of Italian vermouth,*
¼ *gill of Scotch whisky.*

Use the mixing glass. Serve with a little lemon-peel juice squeezed on top.

Boomerang Cocktail

1 *dash of Angostura bitters,*
1 *dash of fresh lemon juice,*
⅙ *gill of French (or dry Martini) vermouth,*
⅙ *gill of Swedish punch,*
⅙ *gill of Canadian Club whisky.*

Use the shaker.

Bosom Caresser Cocktail

3 *dashes of grenadine,*
The yoke of one egg,
⅙ *gill of orange curaçao,*
⅓ *gill of brandy.*

Use the shaker.

Brandy Gump Cocktail

2 *dashes of grenadine,*
The juice of one lemon,
$\frac{1}{2}$ *gill of brandy.*

Use the shaker. Serve with a cherry and a little lemon-peel juice squeezed on top.

Brave Bull Cocktail

$\frac{1}{6}$ *gill of tequila,*
$\frac{1}{6}$ *gill of kalhua.*

Over ice. Use old-fashioned glass.

Brazil Cocktail

1 *dash of Angostura bitters,*
1 *dash of pernod,*
$\frac{1}{4}$ *gill of French vermouth,*
$\frac{1}{4}$ *gill of dry sherry.*

Use the mixing glass. Serve with a little lemon-peel juice squeezed on top.

Bronx Cocktail

The juice of a quarter of an orange,
$\frac{1}{6}$ *gill of French vermouth,*
$\frac{1}{6}$ *gill of Italian vermouth,*
$\frac{1}{6}$ *gill of dry gin.*

Use the shaker.

Brooklyn Cocktail

1 *dash of Amer Picon,*
1 *dash of maraschino,*
$\frac{1}{6}$ *gill of French (or dry Martini) vermouth,*
$\frac{1}{3}$ *gill of Canadian Club whisky.*

Use the mixing glass.

Buck's Fizz Cocktail

> *Juice of an orange,*
> *Top with champagne.*

Use large goblet glass.

B.V.D. Cocktail

> $\frac{1}{6}$ *gill of French vermouth,*
> $\frac{1}{6}$ *gill of bacardi rum,*
> $\frac{1}{6}$ *gill of dry gin.*

Use the shaker.

Byrrh Special Cocktail

> $\frac{1}{4}$ *gill of dry gin,*
> $\frac{1}{4}$ *gill of Byrrh.*

Use the mixing glass.

Café de Paris Cocktail

> 3 *dashes of anisette,*
> *The white of one egg,*
> 1 *teaspoonful of fresh cream,*
> $\frac{1}{2}$ *gill of dry gin.*

Use the shaker.

Café Royal Appetizer Cocktail

> *The juice of half an orange,*
> $\frac{1}{4}$ *gill of Dubonnet,*
> $\frac{1}{4}$ *gill of dry gin.*

Use the shaker.

Calvados Cocktail

For four persons:
⅔ gill of fresh orange juice,
⅓ gill of Cointreau,
⅓ gill of orange bitters,
⅔ gill of calvados.
Use the shaker.

Cardinale Cocktail

⅕ gill of dry gin,
⅒ gill of dry vermouth,
⅒ gill of Campari.
Shake and strain in cocktail glass.

Champagne Cocktail

1 lump of sugar,
2 dashes of Angostura bitters,
2 pieces of lemon peel,
Champagne.
One bottle of champagne will make six cocktails. Put a lump of sugar in a wine-glass, and add the Angostura bitters. Then squeeze the juice of one piece of lemon-peel into the glass. Add an ice cube, and fill with champagne. Stir gently, then squeeze the juice of the other piece of lemon-peel on top, and drop this piece of lemon-peel into the glass.

Champs Elysées Cocktail

1 dash of Angostura bitters,
⅛ gill of Chartreuse,
⅛ gill of sweetened lemon juice,
¼ gill of brandy.
Use the shaker.

Charles Cocktail

1 *dash of Angostura bitters,*
¼ *gill of Italian vermouth,*
¼ *gill of brandy.*
Use the mixing glass.

Cherry Blossom Cocktail

1 *dash of grenadine,*
1 *dash of orange curaçao,*
1 *dash of fresh lemon juice,*
¼ *gill of cherry brandy,*
¼ *gill of brandy.*
Use the shaker. Serve very cold.

Chinese Cocktail

1 *dash of Angostura bitters,*
3 *dashes of Cointreau,*
⅙ *gill of grenadine,*
⅓ *gill of rum.*
Use the shaker.

Chocolate Cocktail (1)

1 *teaspoonful of powdered chocolate,*
1 *egg,*
¼ *gill of yellow Chartreuse,*
¼ *gill of maraschino.*
Use the shaker.

Chocolate Cocktail (2)

1 *teaspoonful of powdered chocolate,*
The yolk of one egg,
¼ *gill of yellow Chartreuse,*
¼ *gill of port.*
Use the shaker.

Claridge Cocktail

$\frac{1}{12}$ gill of apricot brandy,
$\frac{1}{12}$ gill of Cointreau,
$\frac{1}{6}$ gill of French vermouth.
$\frac{1}{6}$ gill of dry gin.

Use the shaker. Serve with a cherry.

Clover Club Cocktail

The white of an egg,
The juice of a fresh lime (or half a lemon),
$\frac{1}{6}$ gill of grenadine,
$\frac{1}{3}$ gill of dry gin.

Use the shaker.

Clover Leaf Cocktail

Prepare as for Clover Club Cocktail, and serve with a sprig of mint on top.

Club Cocktail

1 or 2 dashes of Angostura bitters,
3 dashes of grenadine,
$\frac{1}{2}$ gill of Canadian Club whisky.

Use the mixing glass. Serve with a cherry and a little lemon-peel juice squeezed on top.

Cobblers

See page 85.

Coffees

See page 117.

Collins

See page 101.

39

Commodore Cocktail

2 *dashes of orange bitters,*
3 *dashes of sugar syrup,*
The juice of half a lime or a quarter of a lemon,
$\frac{1}{2}$ *gill of Canadian Club whisky.*

Use the shaker.

Coolers

See page 86.

Cooperstown Cocktail

$\frac{1}{6}$ *gill of French vermouth,*
$\frac{1}{6}$ *gill of Italian vermouth,*
$\frac{1}{6}$ *gill of dry gin,*
2 *sprigs of fresh mint.*

Use the mixing glass. Serve with a cherry on top.

Coronation Cocktail

1 *dash of maraschino,*
2 *dashes of orange bitters,*
$\frac{1}{4}$ *gill of dry sherry,*
$\frac{1}{4}$ *gill of French vermouth.*

Use the mixing glass.

Creole Cocktail

2 *dashes of Amer Picon,*
2 *dashes of Bénédictine,*
$\frac{1}{4}$ *gill of Italian vermouth,*
$\frac{1}{4}$ *gill of Canadian Club whisky.*

Use the mixing glass. Serve with a little lemon-peel juice squeezed on top.

Crow Cocktail

1 *dash of grenadine,*
⅓ *gill of fresh lemon juice,*
⅙ *gill of Scotch whisky.*
Use the mixing glass.

Crustas

See page 88.

Cuba Libre Cocktail

Insert juice and the rind of ½ lime (or lemon) in glass. Add ice,
⅓ *gill of white rum and fill with Coca-Cola.*
Use 10 oz. glass.

Cuban Cocktail

⅛ *gill of fresh lime juice,*
⅛ *gill of apricot brandy,*
¼ *gill of brandy.*
Use the mixing glass.

Cups and Punches

See page 102.

Daiquiri Cocktail

⅓ *gill of white rum,*
⅑ *gill of fresh lime or lemon juice,*
2 *teaspoonsful of sugar.*
Use the shaker.

Daisies

See page 89.

Dandy Cocktail

    1 *dash of Angostura bitters,*
    3 *dashes of Cointreau,*
    1 *piece of lemon peel,*
    1 *piece of orange peel,*
    $\frac{1}{4}$ *gill of Dubonnet,*
    $\frac{1}{4}$ *gill of Canadian Club whisky.*
Use the shaker.

Dempsey Cocktail

    2 *dashes of pernod,*
    3 *dashes of grenadine,*
    $\frac{1}{3}$ *gill of calvados,*
    $\frac{1}{6}$ *gill of dry gin.*
Use the shaker.

Depth Bomb Cocktail

    1 *dash of fresh lemon juice,*
    4 *dashes of grenadine,*
    $\frac{1}{4}$ *gill of calvados,*
    $\frac{1}{4}$ *gill of brandy.*
Use the shaker.

Depth Charge Cocktail

    4 *dashes of fresh lemon juice,*
    2 *dashes of grenadine,*
    $\frac{1}{4}$ *gill of calvados,*
    $\frac{1}{4}$ *gill of brandy.*
Use the shaker.

Diplomat Cocktail

    1 *dash of maraschino,*
    $\frac{1}{3}$ *gill of French vermouth,*
    $\frac{1}{6}$ *gill of Italian vermouth.*
Use the mixing glass. Serve with a cherry and a little lemon-peel
juice squeezed on top.

Doctor Cocktail

$\frac{1}{3}$ *gill of Swedish punch,*
$\frac{1}{6}$ *gill of fresh lime juice (or lemon juice).*
Use the shaker.

Dubonnet Cocktail

$\frac{1}{4}$ *gill of Dubonnet,*
$\frac{1}{4}$ *gill of dry gin.*
Use the mixing glass. Serve with a little lemon-peel juice squeezed on top.

Duchess Cocktail

$\frac{1}{6}$ *gill of French (or dry Martini) vermouth,*
$\frac{1}{6}$ *gill of Italian vermouth,*
$\frac{1}{6}$ *gill of pernod.*
Use the mixing glass.

East India Cocktail

2 *dashes of Angostura bitters,*
2 *dashes of pineapple juice (or maraschino),*
2 *dashes of orange curaçao,*
$\frac{1}{2}$ *gill of brandy.*
Use the shaker. Serve with a cherry and a little lemon-peel juice squeezed on top.

Egg Noggs

See page 110.

Fair and Warmer Cocktail

2 *dashes of orange curaçao,*
$\frac{1}{6}$ *gill of Italian vermouth,*
$\frac{1}{3}$ *gill of bacardi rum.*
Use the mixing glass.

Fairy Belle Cocktail

> 1 *teaspoonful of grenadine,*
> *The white of one egg,*
> $\frac{1}{8}$ *gill of apricot brandy,*
> $\frac{3}{8}$ *gill of dry gin.*

Use the shaker.

Fallen Angel Cocktail

> 1 *dash of Angostura bitters,*
> 2 *dashes of crème de menthe,*
> *The juice of half a lemon,*
> $\frac{1}{2}$ *gill of dry gin.*

Use the shaker.

Fioupe Cocktail

> 1 *teaspoonful of Bénédictine,*
> $\frac{1}{4}$ *gill of Italian vermouth,*
> $\frac{1}{4}$ *gill of brandy.*

Use the mixing glass. Serve with a cherry and a little lemon-peel juice squeezed on top.

Fixes

See page 90.

Fizzes

See page 91.

Flips

See page 111.

44

'Flu Cocktail

> 1 *dash of Jamaica ginger,*
> 3 *dashes of ginger brandy,*
> 3 *dashes of rock candy syrup,*
> *The juice of half a lemon,*
> ½ *gill of Canadian Club whisky.*

Use the mixing glass. Do *not* ice.

Fourth Degree Cocktail

> 4 *dashes of pernod,*
> ⅛ *gill of French vermouth,*
> ⅛ *gill of Italian vermouth,*
> ¼ *gill of dry gin.*

Use the mixing glass. Serve with a cherry.

Fruit and Non-Alcoholic Cocktails

See page 80.

Gibson Cocktail

> *Dry Martini cocktail,*
> *plus cocktail onion.*

Gimlet Cocktail

> ⅓ *gill of dry gin,*
> ⅙ *gill of lime cordial.*

Use the mixing glass.

Gin Cocktail

> 4 *or* 5 *dashes of orange bitters,*
> ½ *gill of dry gin.*

Use the shaker. Serve with a little lemon-peel juice squeezed on top.

Glad Eye Cocktail

$\frac{1}{6}$ gill of crème de menthe,
$\frac{1}{3}$ gill of pernod.
Use the shaker.

Golden Cadillac Cocktail

$\frac{1}{6}$ gill of Galliano,
$\frac{1}{6}$ gill of White curaçao or Cointreau,
$\frac{1}{6}$ gill of cream.
Use the shaker.

Golden Dream Cocktail

$\frac{1}{5}$ gill of Galliano,
$\frac{1}{10}$ gill of Cointreau,
$\frac{1}{10}$ gill of orange juice,
$\frac{1}{10}$ gill of fresh cream.
Shake and serve in champagne glass.

Grand Slam Cocktail

$\frac{1}{8}$ gill of French vermouth,
$\frac{1}{8}$ gill of Italian vermouth,
$\frac{1}{4}$ gill of Swedish punch.
Use the mixing glass.

Grape Vine Cocktail

1 dash of grenadine,
$\frac{1}{8}$ gill of fresh lemon juice,
$\frac{1}{8}$ gill of fresh grape juice,
$\frac{1}{4}$ gill of dry gin.
Use the shaker.

Grasshopper Cocktail

$\frac{1}{6}$ gill of green crème de menthe,
$\frac{1}{6}$ gill of white crème de cacao,
$\frac{1}{6}$ gill of fresh cream.
Shape and serve in champagne glass with straws.

Greenbriar Cocktail

1 *dash of peach bitters,*
$\frac{1}{3}$ *gill of dry sherry,*
$\frac{1}{6}$ *gill of French vermouth,*
1 *sprig of fresh mint.*
Use the mixing glass.

Green Dragon Cocktail

For four persons:
8 *dashes of peach bitters,*
$\frac{1}{4}$ *gill of fresh lemon juice,*
$\frac{1}{4}$ *gill of kummel,*
$\frac{1}{2}$ *gill of crème de menthe,*
1 *gill of dry gin.*
Use the shaker.

Grenadier Cocktail

3 *dashes of grenadine,*
$\frac{1}{4}$ *gill of ginger wine,*
$\frac{1}{4}$ *gill of brandy.*
Use the shaker.

Guard's Cocktail

2 *dashes of orange curaçao,*
$\frac{1}{6}$ *gill of Italian vermouth,*
$\frac{1}{3}$ *gill of dry gin.*
Use the shaker. Serve with cherry.

Harvard Cocktail

1 *dash of sugar syrup,*
2 *dashes of Angostura bitters,*
$\frac{1}{4}$ *gill of Italian vermouth,*
$\frac{1}{4}$ *gill of brandy.*
Use the mixing glass. Serve with a little lemon-peel juice squeezed on top.

Harvey Wallbanger Cocktail

$\frac{1}{3}$ *gill of vodka,*
$\frac{2}{3}$ *gill of orange juice.*

Shake and strain on to ice. Float 2 teaspoons Galliano liqueur.
Serve with straws.

Hawaiian Cocktail

$\frac{1}{3}$ *gill of dry gin,*
$\frac{1}{3}$ *gill of orange juice,*
1 *dash Cointreau.*

Shake.

Highballs

See page 93.

"Hoop La!" Cocktail

$\frac{1}{8}$ *gill of fresh lemon juice,*
$\frac{1}{8}$ *gill of Lillet,*
$\frac{1}{8}$ *gill of Cointreau,*
$\frac{1}{8}$ *gill of brandy.*

Use the shaker.

"Hoots Mon" Cocktail

$\frac{1}{8}$ *gill of Lillet,*
$\frac{1}{8}$ *gill of Italian vermouth,*
$\frac{1}{4}$ *gill of Scotch whisky.*

Use the mixing glass.

Hop Toad Cocktail

$\frac{1}{8}$ *gill of fresh lemon juice,*
$\frac{3}{8}$ *gill of apricot brandy.*

Use the shaker.

Clockwise from top left: Tipperary Cocktail (75), Bentley Cocktail (31), Star Cocktail (73), Prince's Smile Cocktail (64), Angel Face Cocktail (28), Ginger Ale Cup (103), Twelve Miles Out Cocktail (76).

Clockwise from bottom left: Western Rose Cocktail (78), Inca Cocktail (49), Kir Cocktail (51), Brandy Cobbler (85), Grapefruit Drink (106), Club Cocktail (39), Porto Fraise (120).

Hot Deck Cocktail

 1 *dash of Jamaica ginger,*
 ⅛ *gill of Italian vermouth,*
 ⅜ *gill of Canadian Club whisky.*
Use the mixing glass.

Hula-hula Cocktail

 1 *or* 2 *dashes of Cointreau,*
 ⅙ *gill of fresh orange juice,*
 ⅓ *gill of dry gin.*
Use the shaker.

Iced Beverages

See page 108.

Inca Cocktail

 1 *dash of orgeat syrup,*
 1 *dash of orange bitters,*
 ⅛ *gill of dry gin,*
 ⅛ *gill of dry sherry,*
 ⅛ *gill of French vermouth,*
 ⅛ *gill of Italian vermouth.*
Use the mixing glass. Serve with a little lemon-peel juice squeezed on top.

Ink Street Cocktail

 ⅙ *gill of fresh lemon juice,*
 ⅙ *gill of fresh orange juice,*
 ⅙ *gill of Canadian Club whisky.*
Use the shaker.

Jack Kearns Cocktail

1 *dash of fresh lemon juice,*
1 *dash of sugar syrup,*
$\frac{1}{8}$ *gill of bacardi rum,*
$\frac{3}{8}$ *gill of dry gin.*
Use the shaker.

Jack Rose Cocktail

The juice of one lime or half a lemon,
$\frac{1}{8}$ *gill of grenadine,*
$\frac{3}{8}$ *gill of applejack brandy or calvados.*
Use the shaker.

Johnnie Mack Cocktail

3 *dashes of pernod,*
$\frac{1}{6}$ *gill of orange curaçao,*
$\frac{1}{3}$ *gill of sloe gin.*
Use the mixing glass. Serve with a little lemon-peel juice squeezed on top.

Journalist Cocktail

2 *dashes of fresh lemon juice,*
2 *dashes of Cointreau,*
1 *dash of Angostura bitters,*
$\frac{1}{12}$ *gill of French vermouth,*
$\frac{1}{12}$ *gill of Italian vermouth,*
$\frac{1}{3}$ *gill of dry gin.*
Use the shaker.

Juleps

See pages 94–95.

K.C.B. Cocktail

1 *dash of apricot brandy,*
1 *dash of fresh lemon juice,*
$\frac{1}{8}$ *gill of kirsch,*
$\frac{3}{8}$ *gill of dry gin.*

Use the shaker. Serve with a little lemon-peel juice squeezed on top.

Kicker Cocktail

2 *dashes of Italian vermouth,*
$\frac{1}{6}$ *gill of calvados,*
$\frac{1}{3}$ *gill of bacardi rum.*

Use the mixing glass.

King Cole Cocktail

1 *dash of Fernet Branca,*
2 *dashes of sugar syrup,*
$\frac{1}{2}$ *gill of Scotch whisky.*

Use the mixing glass. Decorate with slices of orange and pineapple.

Kir Cocktail

1 *glass of dry white wine,*
1 *teaspoonful of crème de cassis.*

With a teaspoon, float crème de cassis on the wine.

Knickerbocker Cocktail

1 *dash of Italian vermouth,*
$\frac{1}{6}$ *gill of French vermouth,*
$\frac{1}{3}$ *gill of dry gin.*

Use the mixing glass. Serve with a little lemon-peel juice squeezed on top.

Ladies' Cocktail

> 2 *dashes of Angostura bitters,*
> 2 *dashes of pernod,*
> 2 *dashes of anisette,*
> ½ *gill of Canadian Club whisky.*

Use the mixing glass. Serve with a slice of pineapple on top.

Lemonades

See page 106.

Liberty Cocktail

> 1 *dash of sugar syrup,*
> ⅙ *gill of bacardi rum,*
> ⅓ *gill of applejack brandy.*

Use the mixing glass.

Linstead Cocktail

> 1 *dash of absinthe,*
> ¼ *gill of sweetened pineapple juice,*
> ¼ *gill of Scotch whisky.*

Use the shaker. Serve with a little lemon-peel juice squeezed on top.

Little Princess Cocktail

> ¼ *gill of Italian vermouth,*
> ¼ *gill of bacardi rum.*

Use the mixing glass.

London Cocktail

> 2 *dashes of orange bitters,*
> 2 *dashes of sugar syrup,*
> 2 *dashes of pernod,*
> ½ *gill of dry gin.*

Use the mixing glass. Serve with an olive and a little lemon-peel juice squeezed on top.

Lone Tree Cocktail

2 dashes of orange bitters,
⅙ gill of French (or dry Martini) vermouth,
⅙ gill of Italian vermouth,
⅙ gill of dry gin.

Use the shaker. Serve with a cherry.

Lord Suffolk Cocktail

For four persons:
¼ gill of maraschino,
¼ gill of Cointreau,
¼ gill of Italian vermouth,
1¼ gills of dry gin.

Use the shaker. Serve with a little lemon-peel juice squeezed on top.

Los Angeles Cocktail

For four persons:
1 dash of Italian vermouth,
The juice of one lemon,
1 egg,
4 teaspoonfuls of sugar,
2 gills of Canadian Club whisky.

Use the shaker.

Luigi Cocktail

1 teaspoonful of grenadine,
1 dash of Cointreau,
The juice of half a tangerine,
¼ gill of French vermouth,
¼ gill of dry gin.

Use the shaker. Serve with a little lemon-peel juice squeezed on top.

Macaroni Cocktail

$\frac{1}{6}$ gill of Italian vermouth,
$\frac{1}{3}$ gill of absinthe.
Use the mixing glass.

Manhattan Cocktail (dry)

2 dashes of Angostura bitters,
$\frac{1}{4}$ gill of French vermouth,
$\frac{1}{4}$ gill of Canadian Club whisky.
Use the mixing glass. Serve with an olive and a little lemon-peel juice squeezed on top.

Manhattan Cocktail (medium)

2 dashes of Angostura bitters,
$\frac{1}{8}$ gill of French vermouth,
$\frac{1}{8}$ gill of Italian vermouth,
$\frac{1}{4}$ gill of Canadian whisky.
Use the mixing glass. Serve with a cherry and a little lemon-peel juice squeezed on top.

Manhattan Cocktail (sweet)

Prepare as for Manhattan Cocktail (dry), using Italian vermouth instead of French vermouth, and serving with a cherry instead of an olive.

Margarita Cocktail

$\frac{1}{3}$ gill of tequila,
$\frac{1}{3}$ gill of lemon juice (fresh),
$\frac{1}{6}$ gill of Cointreau.
Shake. Edge rim of glass with salt.

Martinez Cocktail

1 *dash of orange bitters,*
2 *dashes of maraschino,*
$\frac{1}{4}$ *gill of French vermouth,*
$\frac{1}{4}$ *gill of dry gin.*

Use the mixing glass. Serve with an olive and a little lemon-peel juice squeezed on top.

Martini Cocktail (dry)

1 *dash of orange bitters,*
$\frac{1}{6}$ *gill of Martini vermouth (dry),*
$\frac{1}{3}$ *gill of dry gin.*

Use the mixing glass. Serve with a little lemon-peel juice squeezed on top.

Martini Cocktail (medium)

$\frac{1}{8}$ *gill of French (or dry Martini) vermouth,*
$\frac{1}{8}$ *gill of Italian vermouth,*
$\frac{1}{4}$ *gill of dry gin.*

Prepare as for Martini Cocktail (dry).

Martini Cocktail (sweet)

$\frac{1}{6}$ *gill of Italian vermouth,*
$\frac{1}{3}$ *gill of dry gin.*

Prepare as for Martini Cocktail (dry).

Mary Pickford Cocktail

3 *dashes of grenadine,*
6 *drops of maraschino,*
$\frac{1}{4}$ *gill of fresh pineapple juice,*
$\frac{1}{4}$ *gill of bacardi rum.*

Use the mixing glass.

Melba Cocktail

2 *dashes of pernod,*
The juice of half a lime or a quarter of a lemon,
2 *dashes of grenadine,*
$\frac{1}{4}$ *gill of Swedish punch,*
$\frac{1}{4}$ *gill of bacardi rum.*

Use the shaker.

Mickie Walker Cocktail

1 *dash of grenadine,*
1 *dash of fresh lemon juice,*
$\frac{1}{8}$ *gill of Italian vermouth,*
$\frac{3}{8}$ *gill of Scotch whisky.*

Use the shaker.

Midnight Cocktail

Prepare as for the Bronx Cocktail, with the addition of one dash of pernod.

Milk Cocktails and Drinks

See pages 110–113.

Millionaire Cocktail (1)

The white of an egg,
2 *dashes of orange curaçao,*
$\frac{1}{6}$ *gill of grenadine,*
$\frac{1}{3}$ *gill of Canadian Club whisky.*

Use the shaker.

Millionaire Cocktail (2)

 1 *dash of grenadine,*
 The juice of one lime,
 $\frac{1}{6}$ *gill of apricot brandy,*
 $\frac{1}{6}$ *gill of rum,*
 $\frac{1}{6}$ *gill of sloe gin.*
Use the shaker.

Mississippi Mule Cocktail

 For four persons:
 $\frac{1}{3}$ *gill of fresh lemon juice,*
 $\frac{1}{3}$ *gill of crème de cassis,*
 $1\frac{1}{3}$ *gills of dry gin.*
Use the shaker.

Monkey Gland Cocktail

 2 *dashes of pernod,*
 2 *dashes of grenadine,*
 $\frac{1}{6}$ *gill of fresh orange juice,*
 $\frac{1}{3}$ *gill of dry gin.*
Use the shaker.

Monte Carlo Imperial Cocktail

 $\frac{1}{8}$ *gill of fresh lemon juice,*
 $\frac{1}{8}$ *gill of white crème de menthe,*
 $\frac{1}{4}$ *gill of dry gin.*
Use the shaker. Strain into a wine-glass, and fill up with champagne.

Mountain Cocktail

 The white of one egg,
 $\frac{1}{12}$ *gill of fresh lemon juice,*
 $\frac{1}{12}$ *gill of French vermouth,*
 $\frac{1}{12}$ *gill of Italian vermouth,*
 $\frac{1}{4}$ *gill of Canadian Club whisky.*
Use the shaker.

Napoleon Cocktail

1 *dash of orange curaçao,*
1 *dash of Fernet Branca,*
1 *dash of Dubonnet,*
½ *gill of dry gin.*

Use the mixing glass. Serve with a little lemon-peel juice squeezed on top.

Negroni Cocktail

⅙ *gill of dry gin,*
⅙ *gill of sweet vermouth,*
⅙ *gill of Campari.*

Stir. Serve with ice and ½ slice of orange.

Newton's Special Cocktail

1 *dash of Angostura bitters,*
⅛ *gill of Cointreau,*
⅜ *gill of brandy.*

Use the mixing glass.

New York Cocktail

1 *lump of sugar,*
The juice of one lime or half a lemon,
2 *dashes of grenadine,*
1 *piece of orange peel,*
½ *gill of Canadian Club whisky.*

Use the shaker. Serve with a little lemon-peel juice squeezed on top.

Nick's Own Cocktail

1 *dash of Angostura bitters,*
1 *dash of pernod,*
¼ *gill of Italian vermouth,*
¼ *gill of brandy.*

Use the mixing glass. Serve with a cherry and a little lemon-peel juice squeezed on top.

Non-Alcoholic Cocktails
See page 80.

"Oh, Henry!" Cocktail
$\frac{1}{6}$ *gill of ginger ale,*
$\frac{1}{6}$ *gill of Bénédictine,*
$\frac{1}{6}$ *gill of Scotch whisky.*
Use the mixing glass.

Old-Fashioned Cocktail
1 *lump of sugar,*
2 *dashes of Angostura bitters,*
$\frac{3}{4}$ *gill of Canadian Club whisky,*
Peel of half a lemon.
Prepare and serve in a tumbler. Put the sugar in first, then add the Angostura bitters, and muddle. Add the whisky and a cube of ice, and stir. Squeeze lemon-peel juice on top, and serve with a piece of lemon-peel in the glass.

Old Pal Cocktail
$\frac{1}{6}$ *gill of French vermouth,*
$\frac{1}{6}$ *gill of Campari,*
$\frac{1}{6}$ *gill of Canadian Club whisky.*
Use the mixing glass.

Olivette Cocktail
3 *dashes of pernod,*
2 *dashes of orange bitters,*
2 *dashes of sugar syrup,*
$\frac{1}{2}$ *gill of Plymouth gin.*
Use the mixing glass. Serve with an olive and a little lemon-peel juice squeezed on top.

One Exciting Night Cocktail

1 *dash of orange juice,*
$\frac{1}{6}$ *gill of French vermouth,*
$\frac{1}{6}$ *gill of Italian vermouth,*
$\frac{1}{6}$ *gill of Plymouth gin.*

Use the shaker. Serve with a little lemon-peel juice squeezed on top.

Opening Cocktail

$\frac{1}{8}$ *gill of grenadine,*
$\frac{1}{8}$ *gill of Italian vermouth,*
$\frac{1}{4}$ *gill of Canadian Club whisky.*

Use the mixing glass.

Oppenheim Cocktail

$\frac{1}{8}$ *gill of grenadine,*
$\frac{1}{8}$ *gill of Italian vermouth,*
$\frac{1}{4}$ *gill of Scotch whisky.*

Use the mixing glass.

Orange Bloom Cocktail

$\frac{1}{8}$ *gill of Cointreau,*
$\frac{1}{8}$ *gill of Italian vermouth,*
$\frac{1}{4}$ *gill of dry gin.*

Use the shaker. Serve with a cherry.

Orange Blossom Cocktail (1)

$\frac{1}{4}$ *gill of fresh orange juice,*
$\frac{1}{4}$ *gill of dry gin.*

Use the shaker.

Orange Blossom Cocktail (2)

    1 *dash of orange bitters,*
    1 *dash of grenadine,*
    $\frac{1}{4}$ *gill of orange juice,*
    $\frac{1}{4}$ *gill of dry gin.*
Use the shaker.

Oriental Cocktail

    The juice of half a lime,
    $\frac{1}{8}$ *gill of Cointreau,*
    $\frac{1}{8}$ *gill of Italian vermouth,*
    $\frac{1}{4}$ *gill of Canadian Club whisky.*
Use the shaker.

Paddy Cocktail

    1 *dash of Angostura bitters,*
    $\frac{1}{4}$ *gill of Italian vermouth,*
    $\frac{1}{4}$ *gill of Irish whisky.*
Use the mixing glass.

Pall Mall Cocktail

    1 *dash of orange bitters,*
    1 *teaspoonful of white crème de menthe,*
    $\frac{1}{6}$ *gill of French vermouth,*
    $\frac{1}{6}$ *gill of Italian vermouth,*
    $\frac{1}{6}$ *gill of dry gin.*
Use the mixing glass.

Palmer Cocktail

    1 *dash of Angostura bitters,*
    1 *dash of fresh lemon juice,*
    $\frac{1}{2}$ *gill of Canadian Club whisky.*
Use the shaker.

Paradise Cocktail

⅙ gill of fresh orange juice,
⅙ gill of apricot brandy,
⅙ gill of dry gin.
Use the shaker.

Parisian Cocktail

⅙ gill of French vermouth,
⅙ gill of crème de cassis,
⅙ gill of dry gin.
Use the mixing glass.

Pegu Club Cocktail

1 dash of Angostura bitters,
1 dash of orange bitters,
3 dashes of lime juice,
⅙ gill of Cointreau,
⅓ gill of dry gin.
Use the mixing glass.

Piccadilly Cocktail

1 dash of pernod,
1 dash of grenadine,
⅙ gill of French vermouth,
⅓ gill of dry gin.
Use the shaker.

Picon Cocktail

¼ gill of Italian vermouth,
¼ gill of Amer Picon.
Use the mixing glass.

Pina Colada

⅙ gill of white rum or tequila,
⅙ gill of coconut cream,
¼ gill of pineapple juice,
1 maraschino cherry.
Use the shaker.

Pink Gin Cocktail

1 *dash of Angostura bitters,*
½ *gill of dry gin.*
Use the shaker.

Pink Lady Cocktail

The white of an egg,
1 *tablespoonful of grenadine,*
½ *gill of dry gin.*
Use the shaker.

Pink Rose Cocktail

1 *teaspoonful of grenadine,*
1 *teaspoonful of fresh lemon juice,*
1 *teaspoonful of sweet cream,*
The white of one egg,
½ *gill of dry gin.*
Use the shaker.

Planter's Cocktail

⅛ *gill of fresh lime juice (or lemon juice),*
⅛ *gill of sugar syrup,*
¼ *gill of rum.*
Use the mixing glass.

Polo Cocktail

The juice of half a lime or quarter of a lemon,
⅓ *gill of French vermouth,*
⅓ *gill of Italian vermouth,*
⅓ *gill of dry gin.*
Use the shaker.

Port Wine Cocktail

    1 *dash of brandy,*
    ½ *gill of port.*

Use the mixing glass. Serve with a little orange-peel juice squeezed on top.

Pousse Cafés

See page 120.

Presto Cocktail

    For four persons:
    4 *dashes of pernod,*
    ⅓ *gill of fresh orange juice,*
    ⅓ *gill of Italian vermouth,*
    1⅓ *gills of brandy.*

Use the mixing glass.

Prince's Smile Cocktail

    1 *dash of fresh lemon juice,*
    ⅛ *gill of apricot brandy,*
    ⅛ *gill of calvados,*
    ¼ *gill of dry gin.*

Use the shaker.

Punches

See page 102.

Quarter Deck Cocktail

    1 *teaspoonful of lime juice,*
    ⅙ *gill of dry sherry,*
    ⅓ *gill of rum.*

Use the mixing glass.

Clockwise from top left: After Supper Cocktail (26), Bobby Burns Cocktail (34), After Dinner Cocktail (26), Stars and Stripes (121), Jersey Lily (121), Hot Scotch (117), Rusty Nail Cocktail (68).

Clockwise from top: Johnnie Mack Cocktail (50), Paddy Cocktail (61), Shamrock Cocktail (70), Whisky Julep (95), Prairie Oyster (84), Irish Coffee (118), Southern Gin Cocktail (centre) (72).

Queen's Cocktail

1 *slice of crushed pineapple*,
$\frac{1}{8}$ *gill of French vermouth*,
$\frac{1}{8}$ *gill of Italian vermouth*,
$\frac{1}{4}$ *gill of dry gin*.

Use the mixing glass.

R.A.C. Cocktail

1 *dash of orange bitters*,
1 *dash of grenadine*,
$\frac{1}{8}$ *gill of French vermouth*,
$\frac{1}{8}$ *gill of Italian vermouth*,
$\frac{1}{4}$ *gill of dry gin*.

Use the mixing glass. Serve with a cherry and a little orange-peel juice squeezed on top.

Raffles Knockout Cocktail

$\frac{1}{3}$ *gill of Kirsch*,
$\frac{1}{3}$ *gill of Cointreau*,
1 *dash of fresh lemon*.

Shake, and serve in champagne glass. Add cherry.

Ray Long Cocktail

1 *dash of Angostura bitters*,
4 *dashes of Pernod*,
$\frac{1}{6}$ *gill of Italian vermouth*,
$\frac{1}{3}$ *gill of brandy*.

Use the mixing glass.

Raymond Hitch Cocktail

The juice of half an orange,
1 *dash of orange bitters*,
1 *slice of pineapple*,
$\frac{1}{2}$ *gill of Italian vermouth*.

Use the shaker.

Resolute Cocktail

$\frac{1}{8}$ *gill of fresh lemon juice,*
$\frac{1}{8}$ *gill of apricot brandy,*
$\frac{1}{4}$ *gill of dry gin.*
Use the shaker.

Rickeys

See page 95.

Rob Roy Cocktail

$\frac{1}{6}$ *gill of Scotch whisky,*
$\frac{1}{6}$ *gill of sweet vermouth,*
1 *dash of Angostura bitters.*
Use the mixing glass. Add cherry.

Roc-a-coe Cocktail

$\frac{1}{4}$ *gill of sherry,*
$\frac{1}{4}$ *gill of dry gin.*
Use the mixing glass. Serve with a cherry.

Rock and Rye Cocktail

1 *piece of rock candy,*
The juice of one lemon,
$\frac{1}{2}$ *gill of Canadian Club whisky.*
Dissolve the rock candy in the whisky, and add the lemon juice.

Rolls-Royce Cocktail

$\frac{1}{6}$ *gill of brandy,*
$\frac{1}{6}$ *gill of Cointreau,*
$\frac{1}{6}$ *gill of orange juice,*
egg white.
Use the shaker.

66

Roosevelt Cocktail

$\frac{1}{6}$ *gill of gin,*
$\frac{1}{6}$ *gill of white rum,*
$\frac{1}{6}$ *gill of lemon juice,*
$\frac{1}{6}$ *gill of grenadine.*
Use the shaker.

Roulette Cocktail

$\frac{1}{8}$ *gill of bacardi rum,*
$\frac{1}{8}$ *gill of Swedish punch,*
$\frac{1}{4}$ *gill of calvados.*
Use the mixing glass.

Royal Clover Club Cocktail

Prepare as for Clover Club Cocktail, using the yolk instead of
the white of an egg.

Royal Cocktail

1 *dash of Angostura bitters,*
1 *dash of orange bitters,*
$\frac{1}{6}$ *gill of Dubonnet,*
$\frac{1}{3}$ *gill of dry gin.*
Use the mixing glass. Serve with a cherry and a little lemon-peel
juice squeezed on top.

Russell House Cocktail

2 *dashes of orange bitters,*
2 *dashes of sugar syrup,*
3 *dashes of blackberry brandy,*
$\frac{1}{2}$ *gill of Canadian Club whisky.*
Use the mixing glass.

Rusty Nail Cocktail

$\frac{1}{6}$ *gill of Drambuie,*
$\frac{1}{3}$ *gill of Scotch whisky.*
Serve in old-fashioned glass on ice.

St. Germain Cocktail

The juice of half a lemon,
The juice of a quarter of a grapefruit,
The white of one egg,
$\frac{1}{2}$ *gill of green Chartreuse.*
Use the shaker.

Sandmartin Cocktail

1 *teaspoonful of green Chartreuse,*
$\frac{1}{4}$ *gill of Italian vermouth,*
$\frac{1}{4}$ *gill of dry gin.*
Use the mixing glass. Serve with a little lemon-peel juice squeezed on top.

Sangarees

See page 96.

Satan's Whiskers Cocktail (straight)

1 *dash of orange bitters,*
$\frac{1}{10}$ *gill of fresh orange juice,*
$\frac{1}{10}$ *gill of French vermouth,*
$\frac{1}{10}$ *gill of Italian vermouth,*
$\frac{1}{10}$ *gill of Grand Marnier,*
$\frac{1}{10}$ *gill of dry gin.*
Use the shaker.

Sazerac Cocktail

1 *lump of sugar,*
1 *dash of Angostura bitters,*
½ *gill of Canadian Club whisky.*

Dissolve the sugar in a teaspoonful of water, and add the bitters and whisky. Stir in the mixing glass, strain, and serve with a dash of absinthe and a little lemon-peel juice squeezed on top.

Scoff-Law Cocktail

For four persons:
4 *dashes of orange bitters,*
⅓ *gill of fresh lemon juice,*
⅓ *gill of grenadine,*
⅔ *gill of French vermouth,*
⅔ *gill of Canadian Club whisky.*

Use the shaker.

Scotch Mist Cocktail

⅓ *gill of Scotch whisky,*
cracked ice,
twist of lemon peel.

Use old-fashioned glass. Shake Scotch whisky with cracked ice and pour unstrained. Add twist of lemon peel. Serve with straws.

Screwdriver Cocktail

⅓ *gill of vodka,*
⅓ *gill of orange juice.*

Serve with ice.

Sensation Cocktail

3 *dashes of maraschino,*
3 *sprigs of fresh mint,*
⅛ *gill of fresh lemon juice,*
⅜ *gill of dry gin.*

Use the shaker.

"S.G." Cocktail

3 *dashes of grenadine,*
$\frac{1}{6}$ *gill of fresh lemon juice,*
$\frac{1}{6}$ *gill of fresh orange juice,*
$\frac{1}{6}$ *gill of Candian Club whisky.*
Use the shaker.

Shamrock Cocktail

3 *dashes of green Chartreuse,*
3 *dashes of green crème de menthe,*
$\frac{1}{4}$ *gill of French vermouth,*
$\frac{1}{4}$ *gill of Irish whisky.*
Use the mixing glass.

Sherry Cocktail (1)

1 *dash of pernod,*
1 *dash of maraschino,*
$\frac{1}{2}$ *gill of dry sherry.*
Use the shaker.

Sherry Cocktail (2)

4 *dashes of orange bitters,*
4 *dashes of French vermouth,*
$\frac{1}{2}$ *gill of dry sherry.*
Use the mixing glass.

Sidecar Cocktail

$\frac{1}{6}$ *gill of fresh lemon juice,*
$\frac{1}{6}$ *gill of Cointreau,*
$\frac{1}{6}$ *gill of brandy.*
Use the shaker.

70

Silver Cocktail

    3 *dashes of maraschino,*
    2 *dashes of orange bitters,*
    $\frac{1}{4}$ *gill of French vermouth,*
    $\frac{1}{4}$ *gill of dry gin.*

Use the mixing glass. Serve with lemon-peel juice squeezed on top.

Silver Streak Cocktail

    $\frac{1}{4}$ *gill of kummel,*
    $\frac{1}{4}$ *gill of dry gin.*

Use the shaker.

Slings

See page 97.

Sloe Gin Cocktail

    $\frac{1}{8}$ *gill of French vermouth,*
    $\frac{1}{8}$ *gill of Italian vermouth,*
    $\frac{1}{4}$ *gill of sloe gin.*

Use the mixing glass.

Smashes

See page 98.

Snowball Cocktail

    $\frac{1}{3}$ *gill of Advocaat,*
    top with lemonade.

Use tall tumbler with ice and garnish with slice of orange and maraschino cherry – serve with straws.

71

Soul's Kiss Cocktail

For four persons:
4 slices of orange,
⅓ gill of fresh orange juice,
⅓ gill of Dubonnet,
⅔ gill of French vermouth,
⅔ gill of Canadian Club whisky.
Use the shaker.

Sours

See page 99.

Southern Gin Cocktail

2 dashes of orange bitters,
2 dashes of Cointreau,
½ gill of dry gin.
Use the shaker. Serve with a little lemon-peel juice squeezed on top.

Spanish Town Cocktail

2 or 3 dashes of Cointreau,
½ gill of rum.
Use the shaker. Serve with a little grated nutmeg on top.

Special Rough Cocktail

1 dash of pernod,
¼ gill of applejack brandy,
¼ gill of brandy.
Use the shaker. Serve very cold.

72

Star Cocktail

1 *dash of French vermouth,*
1 *dash of Italian vermouth,*
1 *teaspoonful of fresh grapefruit juice,*
$\frac{1}{4}$ *gill of calvados,*
$\frac{1}{4}$ *gill of dry gin.*

Use the shaker.

Stinger Cocktail

$\frac{1}{8}$ *gill of white crème de menthe,*
$\frac{3}{8}$ *gill of brandy.*

Use the shaker. Serve very cold.

Summer Beverages

See page 106.

S.W.1 Cocktail

$\frac{1}{6}$ *gill of vodka,*
$\frac{1}{6}$ *gill of Campari,*
$\frac{1}{6}$ *gill of orange juice,*
egg white.

Use the shaker.

Tanglefoot Cocktail

For four persons:
$\frac{1}{3}$ *gill of fresh lemon juice,*
$\frac{1}{3}$ *gill of fresh orange juice,*
$\frac{2}{3}$ *gill of Swedish punch,*
$\frac{2}{3}$ *gill of bacardi rum.*

Use the shaker.

73

Tequila Sunrise Cocktail

$\frac{1}{3}$ *gill of Tequila,*
$\frac{2}{3}$ *gill of orange juice.*

Shake well. Pour into the glass. Add dash of grenadine. Serve with straws.

Third Degree Cocktail

4 *dashes of pernod,*
$\frac{1}{6}$ *gill of French vermouth,*
$\frac{1}{3}$ *gill of dry gin.*

Use the mixing glass. Serve with an olive.

Third Rail Cocktail

1 *dash of pernod,*
$\frac{1}{6}$ *gill of applejack brandy or calvados,*
$\frac{1}{6}$ *gill of brandy,*
$\frac{1}{6}$ *gill of bacardi rum.*

Use the shaker.

Thistle Cocktail

2 *dashes of Angostura bitters,*
$\frac{1}{4}$ *gill of Italian vermouth,*
$\frac{1}{4}$ *gill of Scotch whisky.*

Use the mixing glass.

Three Miller Cocktail

3 *dashes of grenadine,*
1 *dash of fresh lemon juice,*
$\frac{1}{6}$ *gill of bacardi rum,*
$\frac{1}{3}$ *gill of brandy.*

Use the shaker.

Tiger's Tail Cocktail

$\frac{1}{3}$ *gill of pastis,*
$\frac{2}{3}$ *gill of orange juice,*
slice of orange.
Over ice. Use old-fashioned glass.

Tinton Cocktail

$\frac{1}{6}$ *gill of port,*
$\frac{1}{3}$ *gill of applejack brandy.*
Use the mixing glass.

Tipperary Cocktail

3 *dashes of grenadine,*
1 *teaspoonful of fresh orange juice,*
2 *sprigs of mint,*
$\frac{1}{6}$ *gill of Italian vermouth,*
$\frac{1}{3}$ *gill of dry gin.*
Use the shaker.

Toddies

See page 115.

Torpedo Cocktail

1 *dash of dry gin,*
$\frac{1}{6}$ *gill of brandy,*
$\frac{1}{3}$ *gill of calvados.*
Use the mixing glass.

Trinity Cocktail

$\frac{1}{6}$ *gill of French vermouth,*
$\frac{1}{6}$ *gill of Italian vermouth,*
$\frac{1}{6}$ *gill of dry gin.*
Use the mixing glass.

Trocadero Cocktail

> 1 *dash of orange bitters,*
> 1 *dash of grenadine,*
> ¼ *gill of French vermouth,*
> ¼ *gill of Italian vermouth.*

Use the mixing glass. Serve with a cherry and a little lemon-peel juice squeezed on top.

Tuxedo Cocktail

> 1 *dash of pernod,*
> 1 *dash of maraschino,*
> 2 *dashes of orange bitters,*
> ¼ *gill of French vermouth,*
> ¼ *gill of dry gin.*

Use the mixing glass. Serve with a cherry and a little lemon-peel juice squeezed on top.

Twelve Miles Out Cocktail

> ⅙ *gill of bacardi rum,*
> ⅙ *gill of Swedish punch,*
> ⅙ *gill of calvados.*

Use the mixing glass. Serve with a little lemon-peel juice squeezed on top.

Vanderbilt Cocktail

> 2 *dashes of Angostura bitters,*
> 3 *dashes of sugar syrup,*
> ⅛ *gill of cherry brandy,*
> ⅛ *gill of brandy.*

Use the mixing glass.

Velocity Cocktail

> *One slice of orange,*
> ⅓ *gill of Italian vermouth,*
> ⅙ *gill of dry gin.*

Use the shaker.

Vodkatini Cocktail

$\frac{1}{3}$ *gill of vodka,*
$\frac{1}{6}$ *gill of dry vermouth,*
twist of lemon peel.
Use the mixing glass.

Waldorf Cocktail

The juice of half a lime or a quarter of a lemon,
$\frac{1}{6}$ *gill of dry gin,*
$\frac{1}{3}$ *gill of Swedish punch.*
Use the mixing glass.

Washington Cocktail

2 *dashes of Angostura bitters,*
2 *dashes of sugar syrup,*
$\frac{1}{6}$ *gill of brandy,*
$\frac{1}{3}$ *gill of French vermouth,*
Use the mixing glass.

Wax Cocktail

3 *dashes of orange bitters,*
$\frac{1}{2}$ *gill of Plymouth gin.*
Use the mixing glass, and serve with a little orange peel juice
squeezed on top.

Wembley Cocktail

$\frac{1}{6}$ *gill of fresh pineapple juice,*
$\frac{1}{6}$ *gill of French vermouth,*
$\frac{1}{6}$ *gill of Scotch whisky.*
Use the shaker.

Western Rose Cocktail

1 *dash of fresh lemon juice,*
$\frac{1}{8}$ *gill of French vermouth,*
$\frac{1}{8}$ *gill of apricot brandy,*
$\frac{1}{4}$ *gill of dry gin.*

Use the shaker.

West Indian Cocktail

4 *dashes of Angostura bitters,*
3 *dashes of fresh lemon juice,*
3 *dashes of sugar syrup,*
1 *lump of ice,*
$\frac{1}{2}$ *gill of dry gin.*

Stir and serve in the same glass.

White Cocktail

2 *dashes of orange bitters,*
6 *dashes of anisette,*
$\frac{1}{2}$ *gill of dry gin.*

Use the mixing glass. Serve with lemon-peel juice squeezed on top.

White Lady Cocktail

$\frac{1}{8}$ *gill of fresh lemon juice,*
$\frac{1}{8}$ *gill of Cointreau,*
$\frac{1}{4}$ *gill of dry gin.*

Use the mixing glass.

White Lily Cocktail

1 *dash of pernod,*
$\frac{1}{6}$ *gill of Cointreau,*
$\frac{1}{6}$ *gill of bacardi rum,*
$\frac{1}{6}$ *gill of dry gin.*

Use the mixing glass.

White Rose Cocktail

The juice of quarter of an orange,
The juice of half a lime or a quarter of a lemon,
The white of one egg,
$\frac{1}{8}$ *gill of maraschino.*
$\frac{3}{8}$ *gill of dry gin.*
Use the shaker.

Whiz-bang Cocktail

2 *dashes of absinthe,*
2 *dashes of grenadine,*
2 *dashes of orange bitters,*
$\frac{1}{6}$ *gill of French vermouth,*
$\frac{1}{3}$ *gill of Scotch whisky.*
Use the mixing glass.

Wyoming Swing Cocktail

The juice of a quarter of an orange,
$\frac{1}{2}$ *teaspoonful of powdered sugar,*
$\frac{1}{4}$ *gill of French vermouth,*
$\frac{1}{4}$ *gill of Italian vermouth.*
Use the mixing glass. Serve in a wine-glass and top with soda water.

X.Y.Z. Cocktail

$\frac{1}{8}$ *gill of fresh lemon juice,*
$\frac{1}{8}$ *gill of Cointreau,*
$\frac{1}{4}$ *gill of bacardi rum.*
Use the shaker.

Yellow Daisy Cocktail

1 *dash of pernod,*
$\frac{1}{5}$ *gill of French vermouth,*
$\frac{1}{10}$ *gill of Grand Marnier,*
$\frac{1}{5}$ *gill of dry gin.*

Use the shaker. Serve with a cherry.

Yellow Parrot Cocktail

$\frac{1}{6}$ *gill of pernod,*
$\frac{1}{6}$ *gill of yellow Chartreuse,*
$\frac{1}{6}$ *gill of apricot brandy.*

Use the shaker.

Yellow Rattler Cocktail

$\frac{1}{8}$ *gill of fresh orange juice,*
$\frac{1}{8}$ *gill of French vermouth,*
$\frac{1}{8}$ *gill of Italian vermouth,*
$\frac{1}{8}$ *gill of dry gin.*

Use the shaker. Serve with a small crushed pickled onion.

FRUIT AND NON-ALCOHOLIC COCKTAILS

Apricot Cocktail

1 *teaspoonful of fresh lemon juice,*
2 *teaspoonfuls of apricot syrup,*
1 *tablespoonful of cream,*
Apricots,
Pineapple chunks.

Slice the apricots and pineapple chunks, and put in a small bowl. Add the lemon juice and apricot syrup. Ice thoroughly, and serve with cream on top.

From left: Daiquiri Cocktail (41), Rolls-Royce Cocktail (66), Knickerbocker Cocktail (51), Apple Pie Cocktail (29), Whisky Fix (91).

Clockwise from top left: Napoleon Cocktail (58), Whisky Collins (101), Green Dragon Cocktail (47), "Hoop La!" Cocktail (48), Bamboo or Reform Cocktail (1) (31), "Hoots Mon" Cocktail (48), Dubonnet Citron (119).

Bitter Cocktail

The juice of a lemon,
The juice of half an orange,
3 dashes of Angostura bitters.

Use the shaker, half filled with broken ice, and strain into a wine-glass. A little sugar or sugar syrup may be added, according to taste.

Blackcurrant Cocktail

2 teaspoonfuls of powdered sugar,
¼ cupful of blackcurrants,
½ grapefruit.

Cut a hole in the middle of the half-grapefruit, and fill with blackcurrants. Serve with powdered sugar on top.

Cherry Cocktail

1 dash of Angostura bitters,
2 dashes of lime juice,
¼ gill of ginger syrup,
¼ gill of cherry syrup,
2 slices of orange,
4 or 5 stoned cherries,
1 gill of soda water.

Use the mixing glass, half filled with broken ice. Add the Angostura bitters, then the lime juice, ginger syrup, and cherry syrup. Stir well, and strain into a tumbler. Fill up with soda water, and serve with slices of orange and cherries.

Cider Cocktail

1 dash of Angostura bitters,
¾ gill of cider,
½ teaspoonful of sugar syrup.

Use the mixing glass, half filled with broken ice. Stir well, and strain into a wine-glass. Serve with a slice of lemon on top. Non-alcoholic cider may be used.

Gooseberry Cocktail
Prepare as for Blackcurrant Cocktail, using gooseberries instead of blackcurrants.

Grape Cocktail
  1 *dash of Angostura bitters,*
  $\frac{1}{4}$ *gill of grape juice,*
  $\frac{1}{2}$ *gill of sugar syrup,*
  2 *slices of fresh fruit,*
  1 *gill of soda water.*

Use the mixing glass, half filled with broken ice. Add the Angostura bitters, then the grape juice and sugar syrup. Stir well, and strain into a tumbler. Fill up with soda water, and serve with slices of fresh fruit on top.

Grapefruit Cocktail (1)
  1 *grapefruit,*
  1 *small tin of pineapple chunks,*
  2 *bananas,*
  1 *gill of sherry.*

Remove the peel, pulp and pips from the grapefruit, and press it through a sieve. Slice the bananas and pineapple thinly, then add them to the grapefruit purée, in equal quantities, making one pint altogether. Sprinkle castor sugar on the fruit, and pour the sherry over it. Stand on ice for about an hour. Serve in sherbet glasses and decorate with fresh strawberries or glacé fruits.

Grapefruit Cocktail (2)
  $\frac{1}{2}$ *grapefruit,*
  1 *orange,*
  Slices of banana,
  Cranberries,
  1 *tablespoonful of sherry or white wine,*
  The juice of one lemon.

Peel the grapefruit and orange, and break both fruits into sections. Remove the pips and arrange the sections alternately round the sides of a sherbet glass. Add slices of bananas and a few cranberries. Sprinkle with icing sugar, squeeze over it the lemon juice, and finish with the sherry or white wine.

Mixed Fruit Cocktail

Equal amounts of:
  Blackcurrants,
  Raspberries,
  Strawberries;
Sugar to taste,
A little lemon juice.

Mash the fruits to a pulp, and add the sugar. Strain the sweetened juice into the shaker, half filled with broken ice, and add the lemon juice and a little water. Shake well, and strain into a wine-glass.

Oranges and Lemons Cocktail

1 *orange,*
1 *lemon,*
2 *or* 3 *cherries,*
1 *dash of crème de menthe,*
2 *teaspoonfuls of powdered sugar.*

Peel the orange and lemon, separate into sections, and place in a sundae glass. Put the cherries in the middle, and add the crème de menthe. Serve with powdered sugar on top.

Prairie Hen Cocktail

2 *dashes of vinegar,*
1 *teaspoonful of Worcester sauce,*
1 *egg,*
2 *dashes of tabasco sauce,*
Pepper and salt.

Mix all the ingredients except the egg. Then drop the egg in the glass without breaking it.

Prairie Oyster Cocktail

The yolk of one egg,
2 dashes of vinegar,
1 teaspoonful of Worcester sauce,
1 teaspoonful of tomato ketchup.

Mix all the ingredients except the egg-yolk. Then drop the egg-yolk in the glass without breaking it. Serve with a dash of pepper on the top.

Pussy Foot Cocktail

⅓ gill of fresh orange juice,
⅓ gill of fresh lemon juice,
⅓ gill of lime juice,
1 dash of grenadine,
yolk of an egg.

Use the shaker.

Raspberry Cocktail

Prepare as for Blackcurrant Cocktail, using raspberries instead of blackcurrants.

Sundew Cocktail

1 dash of Angostura bitters,
¼ gill of sugar syrup,
¼ gill of grape juice,
½ gill of orange juice,
2 slices of orange,
¾ gill of soda water.

Use the mixing glass. Add the Angostura bitters, then the sugar syrup, orange juice and grape juice. Stir well, and strain into a tumbler. Fill up with soda water, and serve with slices of orange on top.

Chapter III

AMERICAN AND OTHER SUMMER DRINKS

Cobblers

COBBLERS may be prepared with either wines or spirits as bases. In most cases they may be prepared in either mixing glass or shaker, half filled with broken ice; exceptions to this are noted in the recipes below.

Brandy Cobbler

1 *teaspoonful of sugar syrup,*
1 *teaspoonful of brown curaçao,*
1 *gill of brandy.*

Shake or mix well, and strain into a tumbler half full of broken ice. Decorate with slices of orange or lemon.

Champagne Cobbler

3 *or* 4 *dashes of sugar syrup,*
1 *or* 2 *dashes of lemon juice,*
2 *dashes of old brandy,*
1 *gill of champagne.*

Prepare in the mixing glass (*not* the shaker), half filled with broken ice. Stir gently, and strain into a tumbler half full of broken ice. Decorate with fruit, and serve with a straw.

Gin Cobbler

Prepare as for Brandy Cobbler, using gin instead of brandy.

Moselle Cobbler

Prepare as for Champagne Cobbler, using moselle instead of champagne.

Port Cobbler

> 5 *dashes of sugar syrup,*
> 1 *or* 2 *dashes of brandy,*
> ¾ *gill of port.*

Mix well, and strain into a tumbler half full of broken ice. Decorate with fruit, and serve with a straw.

Whisky Cobbler

Prepare as for Brandy Cobbler, using whisky instead of brandy.

Coolers

Coolers are all made in the same way. The drink is prepared and served in a tall glass or tumbler. First put in one lump of ice, and then add the ingredients.

Bulldog Cooler

> 1 *or* 2 *dashes of sugar syrup,*
> *The juice of half an orange,*
> ½ *gill of dry gin,*
> ⅓ *pint of ginger ale.*

Stir well, squeeze a little orange-peel juice on top, and serve.

Club Cooler

> 1 *dash of lemon juice,*
> ⅙ *gill of grenadine,*
> ⅓ *gill of Italian vermouth,*
> ½ *pint of soda water.*

Stir well, squeeze a little lemon-peel juice on top, and serve.

New York Cooler

$\frac{1}{4}$ *gill of lemon squash,*
3 *dashes of grenadine,*
$\frac{1}{2}$ *gill of Canadian Club whisky,*
$\frac{1}{3}$ *pint of soda water.*

Stir well, squeeze a little lemon-peel juice on top, and serve with a slice of lemon.

Remsen Cooler

The juice of half a lemon,
$\frac{1}{2}$ *gill of Remsen's Scotch whisky,*
$\frac{1}{3}$ *pint of ginger ale.*

Stir well, squeeze a little lemon-peel juice on top, and serve.

Rum Cooler

1 *teaspoonful of sugar syrup,*
$\frac{1}{4}$ *gill of lime juice,*
$\frac{1}{2}$ *gill of rum,*
$\frac{1}{3}$ *pint of soda water.*

Stir well, and serve.

Whisky Cooler

2 *dashes of orange bitters,*
$\frac{1}{2}$ *gill of Scotch whisky,*
$\frac{1}{2}$ *pint of soda water.*

Stir well, and serve with a slice of orange. If desired sweeter, include one or two dashes of sugar syrup.

Whiz-bang Cooler

$\frac{1}{2}$ *gill of dry gin,*
$\frac{1}{2}$ *pint of ginger ale.*

Stir well, and serve with a dash of peppermint (crème de menthe) and a sprig of mint on top.

Crustas

All crustas are made in the same way. They are prepared in the shaker, half filled with broken ice, strained into the crusta glass, and decorated with slices of fruit in season.

The crusta glass is about the same size as a small wine-glass, and it has to be specially prepared beforehand. Instructions for this preparation are as follows.

First moisten the inside edges of the glass with lemon juice, and dust with castor sugar to obtain a frosted effect. Now take a clean lemon, cut off the ends, and peel the rest spiral fashion. Place this peel in the crusta glass as a lining.

Bacardi Crusta

1 *teaspoonful of sugar syrup,*
$\frac{1}{6}$ *gill of lemon juice,*
2 *dashes of Angostura bitters,*
1 *teaspoonful of pernod,*
$\frac{1}{3}$ *gill of bacardi rum.*

Brandy Crusta

1 *teaspoonful of sugar syrup,*
$\frac{1}{6}$ *gill of lemon juice,*
1 *dash of Angostura bitters,*
1 *teaspoonful of maraschino,*
1 *dash of orange bitters,*
$\frac{1}{3}$ *gill of brandy.*

Gin Crusta

Prepare as for Brandy Crusta, using dry gin instead of brandy. As a variation, pineapple syrup may be used instead of maraschino.

Rum Crusta

1 *teaspoonful of sugar syrup,*
$\frac{1}{6}$ *gill of lemon juice,*
2 *dashes of Angostura bitters,*
1 *teaspoonful of maraschino,*
$\frac{1}{3}$ *gill of rum.*

Whisky Crusta

Prepare as for Brandy Crusta, using Scotch whisky instead of brandy. Alternatively, Irish whiskey may be used.

Daisies

Daisies are mixed in the shaker, half filled with broken ice, and may be served in two different ways. One is to strain into a wine glass, and the other to strain into a tumbler and fill up with soda water. The quantities given in the recipes below are suitable for serving in tumblers with soda water; if it is wished to serve in wine-glasses without soda water, the quantities should be halved. Daisies may be decorated with slices of fresh fruit on top.

Brandy Daisy

$\frac{1}{4}$ *gill of grenadine,*
$\frac{1}{2}$ *gill of lemon juice,*
$\frac{1}{2}$ *gill of lime juice,*
$\frac{1}{2}$ *gill of brandy.*
Shake well, and strain.

Gin Daisy

$\frac{1}{8}$ *gill of grenadine,*
$\frac{1}{2}$ *gill of lemon juice,*
$\frac{1}{2}$ *gill of dry gin.*
Shake well, and strain

Rum Daisy

$\frac{1}{8}$ *gill of grenadine,*
$\frac{1}{2}$ *gill of lemon juice,*
2 *or* 3 *dashes of maraschino or brown curaçao,*
$\frac{1}{2}$ *gill of rum.*

Shake well, and strain.

Whisky Daisy

$\frac{1}{6}$ *gill of grenadine,*
$\frac{1}{2}$ *gill of lemon juice,*
$\frac{1}{2}$ *gill of lime juice,*
$\frac{1}{4}$ *gill of orange juice,*
$\frac{1}{2}$ *gill of Scotch whisky.*

Shake well, and strain. The flavour may be considered improved if two dashes of brown curaçao are added.

White Horse Daisy

2 *dashes of grenadine,*
$\frac{1}{2}$ *gill of lemon juice,*
1 *teaspoonful of pernod,*
The white of an egg,
$\frac{1}{2}$ *gill of White Horse whisky.*

Shake well, and strain. The flavour may be considered improved if a dash of anisette is added.

Fixes

Fixes are prepared and served in a tumbler. After putting in the ingredients, half fill (or more) the tumbler with finely broken ice, stir, and decorate the top with fruits in season.

Brandy Fix

1 *teaspoonful of sugar syrup,*
The juice of half a lemon,
$\frac{1}{4}$ *gill of brandy,*
$\frac{1}{4}$ *gill of cherry brandy,*
A little water to taste.

Gin Fix

2 teaspoonfuls of sugar syrup,
The juice of half a lemon,
¾ gill of dry gin,
Water to taste.

Rum Fix

Prepare as for Brandy Fix, using rum instead of brandy.

Whisky Fix

Prepare as for Gin Fix, using Scotch whisky instead of gin.

Fizzes

Fizzes are prepared in the shaker, half filled with broken ice, and then strained into a tall glass or tumbler. Fill up with soda water to serve.

Angostura Fizz

⅛ gill of sugar syrup,
¼ gill of Angostura bitters,
½ gill of lemon juice,
The white of an egg.

Brandy Fizz

¾ gill of lemon juice,
5 or 6 dashes of grenadine,
1 teaspoonful of brown curaçao,
The white of an egg,
½ gill of brandy.

Cream Fizz

1 teaspoonful of sugar syrup,
The juice of one lemon,
1 teaspoonful of fresh cream,
¾ gill of dry gin.

Gin Fizz

1 teaspoonful of sugar syrup,
The juice of one lemon, or equal parts of lemon and lime,
¾ gill of dry gin.

Golden Fizz

Prepare as for Gin Fizz, adding the yolk of one egg.

Morning Glory Fizz

½ teaspoonful of sugar syrup,
The juice of half a lemon,
The white of an egg,
2 dashes of pernod,
¾ gill of Scotch whisky.

Orange Fizz

Prepare as for Gin Fizz, using orange juice instead of lemon juice.

Royal Fizz

1 teaspoonful of sugar syrup or grenadine,
The juice of one lemon,
1 egg,
¾ gill of dry gin,

Rum Fizz

Prepare as for Gin Fizz, using rum instead of dry gin.

Rye Fizz

5 or 6 dashes of grenadine,
¾ gill of lemon juice,
The white of an egg,
1 teaspoonful of brown curaçao,
½ gill of Canadian Club whisky.

Silver Fizz

Prepare as for Gin Fizz, adding the white of one egg.

Highballs

Highballs are prepared and served in a tumbler.

Applejack Highball

Put one or two lumps of ice in the tumbler, add $\frac{3}{4}$ gill of applejack brandy, and fill up with soda water or ginger ale. Serve with a piece of lemon peel if desired; alternatively, with a slice of lemon.

Brandy Highball

Gin Highball

Rum Highball

Sherry Highball

Vermouth Highball

Whisky Highball

Prepare each of these as for Applejack Highball, using brandy, dry gin, rum, sherry, French or Italian vermouth, or Scotch (or Irish) whisky instead of applejack brandy.

Other bases, including wines such as claret and apéritif wines such as Dubonnet, may be used to make highballs in the same way.

Mint Juleps

Mint julep is a traditional drink in the southern states of the U.S.A. However, there are many different ways of preparation in use, and there is considerable difference of opinion about their rival merits.

Brandy Julep (1)

First prepare the mint julep glass, which may be an ordinary tumbler. Fill it with finely shaved ice, and put in two or three sprigs of fresh mint, the leaves of which have been dipped in powdered sugar. Decorate with fruit in season.

Now comes the preparation of the julep. Cover four tender sprigs of fresh mint with powdered sugar, and add just enough water to dissolve the sugar. Crush the mint *very gently* for a few minutes, to extract the flavour. Strain into a tumbler, and add broken ice and ¾ gill of brandy. Stir well, and strain into the prepared mint julep glass. Serve with straws.

Brandy Julep (2)

Cover four tender sprigs of fresh mint with powdered sugar, and add just enough water to dissolve the sugar. Crush the mint *very gently* for a few minutes, to extract the flavour. Now put half of the mint and the liquid at the bottom of a pewter tankard. Half fill the tankard with finely shaved ice, add the remainder of the mint and liquid, and fill the tankard with more finely shaved ice.

Now put the tankard in an ice-box or refrigerator, and leave it there for at least two hours. An hour before serving, put in ¾ gill of brandy. When serving, decorate with two or three sprigs of fresh mint the leaves of which have been dipped in powdered sugar. Serve with straws.

Brandy Julep (3)

Cover four tender sprigs of fresh mint with powdered sugar, and add just enough water to dissolve the sugar. Crush the mint very gently, add ¾ gill of brandy, and fill the tumbler with broken ice.

Stir gently, decorate on top with two or three sprigs of mint the leaves of which have been dipped in powdered sugar. Serve with straws.

Champagne Julep

Put one lump of sugar in a tumbler, and add two tender sprigs of fresh mint. Crush the mint very gently, add two lumps of ice, and fill the tumbler with champagne. Stir gently, and decorate with fruit in season.

Gin Julep

Rum Julep

Whisky Julep

Prepare each of these as for Brandy Julep (any of the three methods), using dry gin, rum, or Scotch whisky instead of brandy.

Rickeys

Most rickeys are made in the same way. They are prepared and served in a tumbler containing one lump of ice.

Applejack Rickey

The juice of half a lime,
¾ gill of applejack brandy.
Fill up with soda water, and stir well.

Brandy Rickey

Gin Rickey

Rum Rickey

Sloe Gin Rickey

Whisky Rickey

Prepare each of these as for Applejack Rickey, using brandy, gin, rum, sloe gin, or Scotch whisky instead of applejack brandy.

The flavour of Gin Rickey may be considered improved with the addition of two dashes of grenadine or of raspberry syrup.

Sangarees

Sugar instead of sugar syrup is used in the preparation of sangarees. The sugar is first dissolved in water and then the solution is poured into a tumbler, in which the sangaree itself is prepared and served.

Ale Sangaree

> 1 *tablespoonful of sugar,*
> $\frac{3}{4}$ *gill of water,*
> *Sufficient ale to fill the tumbler.*

Pour out the ale carefully, decorate with grated nutmeg, and serve.

Port Wine Sangaree

> 1 *teaspoonful of sugar,*
> $\frac{1}{2}$ *gill of water,*
> 1 *gill of port.*

Add the port and fill the glass two-thirds full of ice. Stir well, decorate with grated nutmeg, and serve.

Sherry Sangaree

1 *teaspoonful of sugar,*
$\frac{1}{2}$ *gill of water,*
$\frac{3}{4}$ *gill of sherry,*

Add the sherry and half fill the glass with ice. Stir well, decorate with grated nutmeg, and serve.

Whisky Sangaree

Prepare as for Sherry Sangaree, using Scotch whisky instead of sherry, and adding water to taste.

Similar sangarees may be prepared with brandy, dry gin, and rum.

Slings

Gin Sling

$\frac{3}{4}$ *gill of dry gin,*
Sugar syrup according to taste.

Put the ingredients in a tumbler containing a lump of ice. Fill up with water or soda water as desired.

Rum Sling

Prepare as for Gin Sling, using rum instead of dry gin.

Singapore Sling

$\frac{1}{6}$ *gill of lemon juice,*
$\frac{1}{3}$ *gill of gin,*
$\frac{1}{6}$ *gill of cherry brandy.*

Use the shaker.

Straits Sling

The juice of half a lemon,
2 dashes of Angostura bitters,
2 dashes of orange bitters,
⅛ gill of cherry brandy,
⅛ gill of Bénédictine,
½ gill of dry gin.

Put the ingredients in the shaker, half filled with broken ice. Shake well, and strain into a tumbler. Fill up with soda water and serve.

Whisky Sling

Prepare as for Gin Sling, using Scotch whisky instead of dry gin.

Other slings may be prepared in exactly the same way with bases such as applejack brandy, brandy, etc.

Smashes

All smashes are made in the same way, and only one recipe need be given in full.

Brandy Smash

½ lump of sugar,
4 sprigs of fresh mint,
½ gill of brandy.

First dissolve the sugar in a little water (or soda water) in the shaker. Add the sprigs of mint, muddle slightly, and then remove them. Now half fill the shaker with ice and put in the brandy. Shake well, and strain into a wine-glass. Decorate with a sprig of mint or fruit on top, and serve.

Gin Smash

Rum Smash

Whisky Smash

Prepare each of these as for Brandy Smash, using dry gin or rum or Scotch whisky instead of brandy.

Sours

Sours are mixed in the shaker, half filled with broken ice, and strained into wine-glasses for serving.

Applejack Sour

> 2 *dashes of sugar syrup,*
> 1 *dash of grenadine,*
> *The juice of half a lemon (or equal parts of lemon and lime),*
> ½ *gill of applejack brandy or calvados.*

Shake well and strain. If desired, add a little soda water, and decorate with fruit.

Brandy Sour

> 1 *teaspoonful of sugar syrup,*
> *The juice of half a lemon (or equal parts of lemon and lime),*
> ½ *gill of brandy.*

Shake well, and strain. If desired, add a little soda water, and decorate with fruit.

Gin Sour

Rum Sour

Whisky Sour

Prepare each of these as for Brandy Sour, using dry gin, rum, or Scotch whisky instead of brandy.

Toddies (cold)

Brandy Toddy

Put one lump of sugar in a small tumbler, and add just enough water to dissolve it. Then add one lump of ice and ½ gill of brandy. Stir and serve.

Gin Toddy

Rum Toddy

Whisky Toddy

Each of these is prepared as for Brandy Toddy, using dry gin, rum, or Scotch whisky instead of brandy. Toddies with other bases may be prepared in the same way.

Tom Collins and John Collins

The essential difference between Tom Collins and John Collins is in the kind of gin used. Tom Collins gets its name from Old Tom gin, which is distilled from the same source as dry gin but contains a small amount of sugar. In the John Collins, Hollands is used instead.

Similar drinks may be prepared with brandy, rum, and whisky, and these are known simply by the 'family' name – Brandy Collins, Rum Collins and Whisky Collins.

The Collins drinks are prepared in the shaker, half filled with broken ice, and are strained into a tumbler which is filled up with soda water.

Tom Collins

1 teaspoonful of powdered sugar (or sugar syrup),
The juice of one lemon or two limes,
¾ gill of Old Tom gin.

If powdered sugar is used, this must be dissolved in the lemon juice before mixing with the gin.

Dry gin may be used instead of Old Tom, but in that case slightly more sugar or sugar syrup should be used.

John Collins

Prepare in exactly the same way as Tom Collins, but use Hollands instead of Old Tom gin.

Brandy Collins

Rum Collins

Whisky Collins

Prepare each of these as for Tom Collins, using brandy, or rum, or Scotch whisky instead of gin.

Gin Buck (Tom Collins)

The juice and peel of half a lime,
¾ gill of Old Tom gin.

Prepare and serve in a tumbler. Add a cube of ice, and fill up with ginger ale.

If dry gin is used instead of Old Tom, it may be desired to add a dash of sugar syrup. This is a matter of personal taste.

Gin Buck (John Collins)

Prepare as for Gin Buck (Tom Collins), using Hollands instead of Old Tom gin.

Chapter IV

CUPS AND PUNCHES

Cups

MOST cups are prepared in the same way. A big lump of ice is placed in a large jug or bowl, and the ingredients are added. The cup is stirred well, and served in the jug. All the cups described here are sufficient for at least four persons.

Burgundy Cup

 1 *bottle of burgundy,*
 ½ *gill of brandy,*
 ½ *gill of maraschino,*
 ¼ *gill of brown curaçao,*
 2 *or* 3 *dashes of Bénédictine,*
 1 *bottle of soda water.*
Decorate with slices of orange and lemon.

Champagne Cup

 ¼ *gill of curaçao,*
 ¼ *gill of maraschino,*
 ½ *gill of brandy,*
 1 *bottle of champagne,*
 1 *bottle of soda water.*
Decorate with slices of lemon and orange and a sprig of fresh mint.

Cider Cup (1)

1 *gill of brandy,*
The juice of one lemon,
One orange (in slices),
1 *quart of cider,*
1 *bottle of soda water.*

Cider Cup (2)

$\frac{1}{3}$ *gill of Cointreau,*
$\frac{1}{4}$ *gill of maraschino,*
$\frac{1}{2}$ *gill of brandy,*
$\frac{3}{4}$ *gill of dry sherry,*
1 *teaspoonful of lemon juice,*
1 *quart of cider.*

Decorate with slices of lemon and orange and a sprig of fresh mint.

Claret Cup

$\frac{1}{4}$ *gill of Cointreau,*
$\frac{1}{2}$ *gill of brandy,*
1 *teaspoonful of lemon juice,*
1 *bottle of claret,*
1 *bottle of soda water.*

Decorate as for Champagne Cup.

Ginger Ale Cup (non-alcoholic)

$\frac{1}{2}$ *lb. of loaf sugar,*
1 *quart of boiling water,*
$\frac{1}{2}$ *teacupful of lime juice,*
1 *bottle of ginger ale.*

First dissolve the sugar in the boling water, then ice and add the other ingredients. Decorate with sprigs of fresh mint.

Hock Cup

¼ *gill of kummel,*
½ *gill of brandy,*
⅛ *gill of yellow Chartreuse,*
¼ *gill of maraschino,*
1 *bottle of hock,*
1 *pint of soda water.*

Decorate as for Champagne Cup.

Moselle Cup

Prepare as for Hock Cup, using moselle instead of hock.

Punches (cold)

When Punch is served cold it is usually prepared in the shaker half filled with broken ice. Shake well, and strain into a tumbler Decorate with fruits in season or sprigs of mint.

Brandy Punch

The juice of half a lemon,
1 *tablespoonful of sugar syrup,*
2 *or* 3 *dashes of Cointreau,*
¾ *gill of brandy.*

Champagne Punch

The juice of half a lemon,
1 *tablespoonful of sugar syrup,*
1 *tablespoonful of Cointreau,*
Balance of champagne.

Shake all except the champagne, and in this case strain into a wine-glass, then fill up with champagne.

Claret Punch

Prepare as for Champagne Punch, using claret instead of champagne.

Gin Punch

The juice of half a lemon,
1 *tablespoonful of sugar syrup,*
2 *or* 3 *dashes of maraschino,*
$\frac{3}{4}$ *gill of dry gin.*

Planter's Punch

The Jamaican classical formula runs: "One of sour (lime), two of sweet (sugar), three of strong (rum), four of weak (ice and water)." There are many variations, but the original is still the best.

Rum Punch

The juice of half a lemon,
1 *tablespoonful of sugar syrup,*
$\frac{3}{4}$ *gill of rum.*
Curaçao or grenadine may be used instead of sugar syrup.

Shandy Gaff

$\frac{1}{2}$ *pint of ale,*
$\frac{1}{2}$ *pint of ginger ale.*
Mix in a tumbler and serve ice cold.

Chapter V

SUMMER BEVERAGES (NON-ALCOHOLIC)

Lemonades, Orangeades, etc.

Ginger Lemonade

The juice of one lemon,
Ginger ale,
Sugar to taste.

Put a lump of ice in a long glass, and add the strained lemon juice, with sugar to taste, and fill up with ginger ale.

Grapefruit Drink

1 grapefruit,
3 oranges,
¼ lb. of loaf sugar,
1 bottle of soda water.

Rub the loaf sugar on the rind of the oranges and then put it in a large jug. Pour over it one pint of water, the strained juice of the oranges and of the grapefruit. Strain, add a lump of ice and some soda water to serve.

Grapefruit and Orangeade

2 grapefruits,
1 gill of orange juice,
1 gill of cider (non-alcoholic),
¼ lb. of loaf sugar,
Soda water.

Put the orange juice and the juice of the grapefruit into a saucepan with the sugar, and boil until the syrup thickens. Then pour into a jug, allow to cool, and add the cider. Serve as for Fruit Syrups.

Lemonade (1)

1 *lemon,*
Sugar to taste.

Squeeze the lemon juice, add the sugar and iced water, and strain into a glass. Serve with ice.

Lemonade (2)

1 *lemon,*
Loaf sugar to taste.

Scrape the rind from the lemons by means of the loaf sugar, and put the sugar into a jug. Pour boiling water over it, one gill for each lemon: squeeze the juice from the lemon and add to the contents of the jug. Boil it all together, adding enough sugar to make a syrup. When it thickens, allow to cool, then strain and add an equal quantity of iced water. Serve.

Limeade

3 *limes,*
Sugar to taste.

Prepare as for Lemonade (1).

Orangeade (1)

4 *oranges,*
$\frac{1}{4}$ *lb. of loaf sugar,*
Soda water.

Thinly peel the oranges, and put the peel into a jug. Add the sugar and half a pint of boiling water. Strain the juice from the oranges into the jug, and allow to cool. Strain, and serve as for Fruit Syrups.

Orangeade (2)

4 oranges,
2 lemons,
2 lb. of loaf sugar.

Scrape the rinds from the oranges and lemons by rubbing with the loaf sugar. Put the sugar in a jug, and pour two quarts of boiling water over it. Add the juice of the oranges and lemons, stir well, and allow to cool. Strain and serve.

Pineapple Lemonade

1 small tin of pineapple chunks,
2 lemons,
¼ lb. of loaf sugar.

Remove the rind from the lemons and put it in a jug. Add one pint of boiling water, the syrup from the tin of pineapple, and the pineapple cut very small. Squeeze the juice from the lemons, mix it with the sugar, and add to the contents of the jug. Allow to stand for three hours, then strain and add soda water and ice before serving.

Raspberry Lemonade

1 lb. of raspberries,
2 lemons,
¼ lb. of castor sugar.

Press the raspberries through a sieve, add the juice of the lemons and the sugar, stir well, and mix with one quart of cold water. Serve with ice.

Iced Beverages

Iced Chocolate

1 pint of chocolate,
Vanilla ice cream.

Make the chocolate in the normal way, and allow it to cool, then stand in a jug surrounded with ice or put in the refrigerator. When required, serve in small glasses topped with vanilla ice cream.

Iced Coffee

Make the coffee in the usual way, allowing two dessertspoonfuls for each person. Strain, and add a little sugar, then leave to cool and ice. Serve topped with whipped cream.

Iced Tea

Make the tea in the usual way, allowing one teaspoonful of tea to half a pint of water. Allow it to draw, then strain and leave to cool. Add a little sugar if desired, and some slices of lemon or fresh fruit juice: then stand on ice until required. Serve with small ice cubes.

Chapter VI

EGG NOGGS, FLIPS, AND MILK PUNCHES

Egg Noggs

EGG noggs may be served cold or hot. If cold, they are prepared in the shaker, half filled with broken ice, and strained into a tumbler. If hot they are prepared in a similar way, but with boiling water instead of cold milk and ice. Only fresh eggs should be used, and the milk should be rich. Serve with grated nutmeg on top.

Baltimore Egg Nogg

1 *egg*
1 *teaspoonful of sugar syrup,*
$\frac{3}{4}$ *gill of madeira,*
$\frac{1}{4}$ *gill of brandy,*
$\frac{1}{4}$ *gill of rum,*
Balance of milk.

Breakfast Egg Nogg

1 *egg,*
$\frac{1}{4}$ *gill of orange curaçao,*
$\frac{3}{4}$ *gill of brandy,*
Balance of milk.

Plain Egg Nogg

1 egg,
1 teaspoonful of sugar syrup,
¾ gill of brandy or rum,
Balance of milk.

Gin or whisky may be used instead of brandy or rum.

Port Wine Egg Nogg

1 egg
1 teaspoonful of sugar syrup,
¾ gill of port,
¼ gill of brandy,
¼ gill of rum,
Balance of milk.

Flips and other Egg Drinks

Ale Flip

The yolk of one egg,
½ pint of ale (preferably bitter),
1 tablespoonful of sugar.

This may be prepared cold (in the shaker, half filled with broken ice) or hot (by heating the ale). Serve with grated nutmeg on top.

Brandy Flip

The yolk of one egg,
½ gill of brandy,
Sugar or sugar syrup to taste.

Prepare in the shaker, half filled with broken ice. Shake well, and strain into a wine-glass: serve with grated nutmeg on top.

Egg Lemonade (non-alcoholic)

The juice of one lemon,
1 oz. of castor sugar,
1 egg,
Ice.

Prepare in the mixing glass, stir well, and strain into a tumbler. Serve with water or soda water.

Egg Punch (non-alcoholic)

1 egg,
1 tablespoonful of vanilla syrup,
Ice,
Balance of milk and soda water.

Beat the egg in a basin, and add vanilla syrup and chopped ice. Shake in the shaker, and strain into a long glass. Add the milk to three-quarter fill the glass, then fill up with soda water.

Egg Sour

1 egg,
¼ gill of Cointreau,
¼ gill of brandy,
3 dashes of lemon juice,
Sugar or sugar syrup to taste.

Prepare in the shaker, half filled with broken ice. Shake well, and strain into a wine-glass.

Port Wine Flip

Rum Flip

Sherry Flip

Whisky Flip

Prepare each of these as for Brandy Flip, using port, rum, sherry or whisky instead of brandy.

Milk Punch and other Drinks

Milk Punch (1)

$\frac{3}{4}$ *gill of brandy,*
3 *dashes of lemon juice,*
1 *tablespoonful of sugar syrup,*
Balance of milk.

This may be prepared cold (in the shaker, half filled with broken ice) or hot (by heating the milk). Serve with grated nutmeg on top.

Milk Punch (2)

$\frac{1}{2}$ *gill of brandy,*
$\frac{1}{4}$ *gill of rum,*
1 *tablespoonful of sugar syrup,*
Balance of milk.

Prepare as for Milk Punch (1).

Milk Shake (non–alcoholic)

1 *egg,*
1 *glass of milk,*
Sugar or sugar syrup to taste.

Prepare in the shaker, half filled with broken ice. Shake well, and strain into a tumbler. The drink may be flavoured with fruit syrup.

Scotch Milk Punch

Prepare as for Milk Punch (1), using Scotch whisky instead of brandy.

Chapter VII

HOT DRINKS

Punches

HOT punches are prepared in the punch bowl and served in punch glasses or cups.

Hot Tea Punch

> 3 *pints of freshly brewed tea,*
> 1 *pint of brandy,*
> 1 *bottle of rum,*
> *Sugar to taste.*

Mix well, and mull with a red-hot poker. Decorate with orange and lemon peel. This should be enough for at least twelve persons.

Oxford Punch

> 3 *parts of rum,*
> 2 *parts of brandy,*
> 1 *part of lemon squash,*
> 6 *parts of boiling water,*
> *Sugar to taste.*

This is a modern version of a traditional recipe. It can be used for any number of persons, provided that the proportions of the ingredients are kept the same.

Toddies

Hot toddies are prepared and served in a tumbler.

Apple Toddy

1 *teaspoonful of sugar,*
1 *baked apple,*
¾ *gill of applejack brandy.*

Strain the juice of the apple into the tumbler, add the sugar and sufficient hot water to dissolve it. Then add the applejack brandy, and fill up with boiling water. Serve with grated nutmeg on the top.

Rum Toddy

1 *teaspoonful of sugar,*
3 *dashes of lime juice,*
¾ *gill of rum.*

Dissolve the sugar in hot water, and add the lime juice and rum. Fill up with boiling water. Serve with grated nutmeg or powdered cinnamon on the top.

Whisky Toddy

1 *teaspoonful of sugar,*
¾ *gill of Scotch whisky.*

Dissolve the sugar in hot water, and add the whisky. Fill up with boiling water. Serve with a slice of lemon on top.

Other Hot Drinks

Ale Posset

1 *pint of milk,*
1 *cupful of sherry,*
1 *cupful of ale,*
4 *lumps of sugar.*

Heat the milk until it almost boils. Meanwhile mix the sherry, ale, and sugar in a jug, and to this add the hot milk. Serve with grated nutmeg.

Blackcurrant Tea (non-alcoholic)

1 *tablespoonful of blackcurrant jelly,*
1 *dessertspoonful of lemon juice,*
4 *lumps of sugar.*

Mix together in a jug, and add a tumblerful of boiling water. Stir well, and stand the jug in a pan of boiling water for twenty minutes. Then strain and serve.

Hot Buttered Rum

2 *tablespoonfuls of rum,*
2 *teaspoonfuls of sugar,*
2 *teaspoonfuls of butter,*
$\frac{1}{2}$ *teaspoonful of mixed spices (cinnamon and cloves).*

Put the ingredients in a tumbler, fill up with boiling water, and stir well.

Hot Fruit Drinks

Fruit syrup,
The juice of one lemon,
Sugar to taste.

Dilute one part of fruit syrup with two parts of hot water, add the sugar and lemon juice, and serve.

Hot Gin

The juice of one lemon,
2 *lumps of sugar,*
$\frac{1}{2}$ *gill of dry gin.*

Prepare as for Hot Buttered Rum.

Hot Lemonade (non-alcoholic)

The juice of one lemon,
Sugar to taste.

Prepare as for Hot Buttered Rum.

Hot Orangeade

2 oranges,
The juice of one lemon,
Sugar to taste.

Peel one orange very thinly, and then boil the peel in half a pint of water for ten minutes. Add the juice of the two oranges and the lemon juice, with sugar to taste. Strain and serve.

Hot Scotch

Prepare as for Hot Gin, using Scotch whisky instead of dry gin.

Port Wine Negus

1 wine-glassful of port wine,
1 lemon,
Sugar to taste.

Put the wine in a long glass, and add the sugar and the rind and juice of the lemon. Fill up with boiling water, and strain.

Coffees

Calypso Coffee

⅙ gill of Tia Maria,
⅙ gill of light rum.

Serve in a wine glass. Fill with hot coffee and top with double cream.

Gaelic Coffee

Hot coffee,
2 teaspoonsful of sugar,
⅓ gill of Scotch whisky,
fresh cream.

Pour fresh cream over back of warmed spoon very gently. DO NOT STIR.

Irish Coffee

Hot coffee,
2 teaspoonsful of sugar,
⅓ gill of Irish whiskey,
fresh cream.

Pour fresh cream over back of warmed spoon very gently. DO NOT STIR.

Chapter VIII

MISCELLANEOUS DRINKS

Apéritifs

APÉRITIF is a French word meaning 'appetizer', and this drink is consumed in France before luncheon and dinner.

Special wines are used in preparing apéritifs, and most of these have trade names, such as Byrrh, Cinzano, Dubonnet, etc. They are ordinary red or white wines with the addition of certain aromatic herbs. Many of the recipes for these special wines are secrets as closely guarded as those used in the manufacture of perfume.

The wines are drunk neat as well as in the long apéritif drinks.

There are literally hundreds of different apéritif combinations, but the majority of them follow a common formula: three parts of the base with one part of fruit syrup. The drink is prepared and served in the same glass. The base and syrup are poured in, water or soda water is added, together with a lump of ice, and the drink is stirred.

Byrrh Cassis

$\frac{1}{2}$ *gill of Byrrh,*
$\frac{1}{6}$ *gill of cassis (blackcurrant)*

An alternative may be prepared by using French vermouth instead of Byrrh.

Dubonnet Citron

$\frac{1}{2}$ *gill of Dubonnet,*
$\frac{1}{6}$ *gill of sirop de citron (lemon).*

Alternatives to Dubonnet include Amer Picon, Byrrh, and Mandarin.

Picon Grenadine

½ *gill of Amer Picon,*
⅙ *gill of grenadine (pomegranate).*
An alternative may be prepared by using French vermouth instead of Amer Picon.

Porto Fraise

½ *gill of port,*
⅙ *gill of fraisette (strawberry).*
An alternative may be prepared by using French vermouth instead of port.

Pousse Cafés

Pousse cafés are served in the glasses of the same name. Each drink consists of a number of liqueurs. No mixing or shaking is required: indeed, the art of preparing a pousse café is in keeping the liqueurs entirely separated from one another by careful pouring. It will be seen that this can be achieved only if the heaviest liqueurs are put in first, and so the order of ingredients is most important. On no account should the drink be stirred.

Amour Pousse

3 *dashes of grenadine,*
The yolk of an egg,
⅙ *gill of maraschino,*
⅙ *gill of old brandy.*

Golden Slipper

The yolk of an egg,
⅙ *gill of yellow Chartreuse,*
⅙ *gill of eau de vie de Danzig (or old brandy).*

Jersey Lily

Equal parts of:
Yellow Chartreuse,
Old brandy.

Knickerbein

The yolk of a fresh egg,
$\frac{1}{6}$ gill of orange curaçao,
$\frac{1}{6}$ gill of kummel,
3 dashes of Angostura bitters.

Stars and Stripes

Equal parts of:
Crème de cassis,
Maraschino,
Green Chartreuse.

Union Jack

Equal parts of:
Grenadine,
Maraschino,
Green Chartreuse.

Chapter IX

CHOOSING AND SERVING WINES

IN general, wines are named after their native districts. The character of a wine does not depend only on the species from which it is made: it depends also on climate and soil. Thus if a champagne vine, for example, were transplanted to another part of the world, or even to another district of France, the grapes harvested from it would not produce what we know as real champagne.

Generally speaking, wine improves with age. The fermentation continues after bottling, and the wine mellows and develops its bouquet. However, there is a limit to the period of improvement, which is eventually followed by deterioration of quality. The effect of age varies considerably from one wine to another. Champagne is perhaps at its best between the ages of six and sixteen: some still wines may go on improving for many more years; yet Rhine wines begin to deteriorate at a very early age.

Wines are often listed with the year of their vintage, and this date is of great importance to the connoisseur. Climate varies from year to year, and so, therefore, does the quality of the vintage. Generally speaking, a dry, sunny summer, with plenty of sunshine towards the end of the season, favours the vines and their grapes: but this is only a rough approximation of a number of factors.

Table Wines

Table wines, which are the wines drunk with food, are commonly of two varieties: red and white. The former are made from red grapes and the latter from white. In French wines there is a third variety, called *rosé*, or pink: this is made either from red and white grapes together, or from a small grape of a colour between the two.

The best-known French table wines are Burgundy and Bordeaux, and there are red and white varieties of both. Famous red Burgundies include Beaune, Chambertin, and Nuits Saint-Georges, while Bordeaux is renowned for the white Barsac, Graves, and Sauternes and the red Médoc. There are many other varieties of both wines. There are several more famous wine-growing regions in France, including Anjou and Alsace.

Rhine and German wines are mostly white. Italy produces both red and white wines, the best known being red Chianti. Hungary is famous for red Tokay.

Fortified Wines

Fortified wines contain much more alcohol than table wines, and do not deteriorate so quickly when exposed to air. They are generally heavier and sweeter, and therefore are not usually drunk with a meal.

Many of these fortified wines are of Spanish origin. Sherry is named after the Spanish district of Jerez. There are two kinds of sherry: dry, which is pale in colour: and brown, which is much sweeter.

Other fortified wines include Port, named after Oporto, in Portugal, and madeira, muscatel, malaga, and marsala. All of these are relatively sweet.

Storing Wines

Wines should be kept in a cellar at an even temperature of about fifty-five degrees. Bottles should be placed on their sides with the heads slightly raised. In this way the corks are kept moist, and there is less danger of air getting into the bottle.

How to Serve Wines

As a general rule, white wines should be chilled and red wines at room temperature. It is a good idea to uncork red wines and place them in the room an hour or so before they are needed.

Champagne is usually served in an ice bucket.

Dry sherry may be slightly chilled, but brown sherry should be served at room temperature.

Great care should be taken not to over-chill wines, or there may be loss of the bouquet. Ice should never be put into wine.

In pouring wines, it is customary for a little wine to be poured into the host's glass first. The reason for this is that there may be a little sediment or pieces of cork at the top of the bottle. The glasses of the guests are filled next, and the host's glass is filled when everyone else has been served.

Wine-glasses should be only three-quarters filled.

There is nothing specially difficult about opening champagne, so long as the object is a good drink and not a firework display. The noise of the pop is no guide to the quality of the champagne. Any bottle of fair champagne, left unchilled and given a good shake-up, will go off with a wonderful bang. But those who judge champagne by the taste, and prefer a full glass to a reduced portion, are advised to reduce the risk of waste by opening the bottle carefully, with the least possible movement, and removing the cork without any pop at all.

When to Serve Wines

With table wines the general rule is to serve red wine with red food and white wine with white food. Thus white wine is served with fish and boiled fowl: red wine with "red" meat and roast fowl and game. Champagne is an exception, and may be served throughout the meal.

Wine should not be served with salads or fruit.

Dry sherry may be served before a meal, instead of the cocktail or apéritif, or with the soup. A relatively dry madeira may be served with the soup, but otherwise fortified wines should not be served until the dessert. Cheese may be eaten with red table wine, port, brown sherry, or madeira, but again care should be taken to see that the dessert wines are not too sweet.

Dessert wines may be drunk with coffee, but here liqueurs may be preferred. There is a wide range of liqueurs, including fine brandies and such popular drinks as cherry brandy, Bénédictine, and Grand Marnier. An ordinary liqueur brandy may be poured into black coffee, but this should never be done with a *fine* or any other liqueur.

Liqueurs are best served in special large glasses, which can be warmed with the hands while the wine is moved in the glass, thus releasing the bouquet.